Martin Nicholas Kunz · Scott Michael Crouch

| NORTH AMERICA | SOUTH AMERICA | AFRICA | EUROPE | | ASIA | AUSTRALASIA |

best designed hotels in europe II countryside locations

W 180° 165° 150° 135° 120° 105° 90° 75° 60° 45° 30° 15° 0° 15° 30° 45° 60° 75° 90° 105° 120° 135° 150° 165° 180° E

avedition *lebensart*

Seaham

Helgoland

Dassow | Nakenstorf

Schneverdingen

Bath

Saint Mawes

Hornbach

Laachen | St. Anton

Lagarde

Laax | Pontresina

Bouliac

Laguiole

Amares

Cattolica

St. Tropez

Arezzo

Crato

Cascais

Arraiolos

Alcácer do Sal

Ibiza | Mallorca

Madeira

Tenerife

Ürgüp

A place of inspiration

A pneumatic drill booms with regular, gun-fire thuds. Still hung-over, a young guest swigs greedily from a bottle of cola at his bedside, and stumbles towards the window, falling full speed over the blue-green duvet ripped hastily from the bed the night before; a heavy, crumpled mass, patterned with delightful yellow and red flowers, frilled along the edge. It's already 12 noon, and his left hand manages to grip the heavy, dark-brown curtain that momentarily brakes his fall. But not for long. With an audible rasp, six plastic rings pop from the dusty hanging rail, and he's lying, bruised and baffled, on the red nylon carpet as the sun finally makes its entrance into the room. Warm, bright sunshine. His eyes squint, he grimaces and struggles to his feet, opening the other curtain in a more orthodox fashion, and pulling the sliding door to the balcony. A quick glance at the clock — thank God the double-glazing keeps out noise. Outside sounds like a combination of Istanbul, Bombay and São Paulo played through loudspeakers. Car horns, tyre screeches, thundering motorbikes, hammering, power saws and the pneumatic drill. The guest's horizontal view ends at the concrete wall opposite, and below lies an exhaust-gas-filled street… although from twelve storeys up, the smell

isn't too bad. Anyway, 14 days in Benidorm on Spain's Costa Blanca, you just make the most of it, huh? And who cares when most of the day is spent in a bar, drinking real English beer, or real German pils? From behind, two hands roughly massage the young man's neck as he earnestly attempts to continue sleeping on the balcony railings. "Come on", says a slightly niggled female voice. "I want to get to the beach while it's still nice and hot. I'm still sooo white, I can't believe it!" remarks his very pink companion.

When journalist, Anke Cimbal, wrote on the theme "Lifestyle and Design Hotels" for the German travel trade magazine "NGZ – Der Hotelier" in spring 2002, she was probably thinking just as little about Benidorm's monstrosities as all the other factory hotels that share their confused, "pick 'n' mix" style. Her headline, "Shrill Refuge" (Schrille Refugien) could, however, fit to 90% of all hotels that try to please with a brash or simply tasteless design. Refuge? Maybe not, but shrill because their attempts to harmonize colour and form are nearly always a half-tone out. A thick glass ashtray that has no relation to the accompanying spotted ceramic vase, for example; or fresh spring flowers that are cancelled out by a savage floral

rug. Clever little black-framed abstract prints that seem to ignore the light nutwood side tables. Even chrome toilet paper holders that refuse completely to make friends with pale blue loo seats. All this may well sound like exaggeration, but is in reality a normal picture of many hundreds of thousands of hotels around the world. The visual equivalent of forcing guests to listen to Britney Spears, Mozart and Dizzy Gillespie all at once. Are you getting a headache yet? The chances are that most people would simply keel over at this kind of an audio stamina test, some may go so far as to consider it torture. The difference between sight and sound might well be that our eyes get used to ugliness much quicker, which deadens its effect. They have, after all, the benefit of built in blinds which can be closed, cutting out displeasing images. That as it may be, the forbearance of our organs of sight is certainly no reason to renounce good design, rather than building us an aesthetic environment. One can dampen the racket from a pneumatic drill, or build quieter cars and aeroplanes, but they will always produce some kind of noise; there is no other way. But who or what drives people to build boring, or downright gruesome hotels?

01 | Stairway in the finca Son Gener, Mallorca. The owner and architect Antonio Esteva has created an aesthetic jewel.

02 | Swimming pool at Son Bernadinet, Mallorca.

04 | Al fresco dining at Villa Fontelunga, Tuscany.

03 | Country idyll in Gascony. The former investment banker and designer, Frédéric Coustols, has restored an entire village.

05 | Relaxing in Mecklenburg-Vorpommern. Architect couple, Johanne and Gernot Nalbach, have realized their personal dream hotel.

It might be the case that the quoted journalist gained many of her notions of "Design" from the staged fantasies of Philippe Starck. Many regard his creations as a synonym for "styled hotels". It this instance "shrill" would not be a completely false adjective, or perhaps "sharp". Those that look carefully will see a system. His interiors show not just an overall concept, but also tell a story, in virtuoso manner – a use of tones, forms and materials that is never imprecise or left to chance. Altogether though, these hotels remain a niche within a niche, within which the media still likes to rummage around, looking for all kinds of possible meanings and ideas. One of the resulting (incorrect) theories equates design with a lack of function, reducing architecture and design to shallow cosmetics. An ongoing misunderstanding that likes to sprout various branches. Before long, the conclusion is reached that whatever is shrill, loud or brash is "Design". If we follow such logic to its conclusion, then our

friend in Benidorm is likely to have been residing in a true temple of design, even if the multi-coloured clash of elements in his quarters was reminiscent of rubbish thrown into a bin. "Refuse Refuge" perhaps?

"Aethstetics have priority over functionality. When one starts making concessions, then the whole picture can be toppled", was the opinion of one prominent hotel manager. If a designer has no desire for function, and wins over his employer with wonderful words, or some other drug, it is little wonder that such sentences are uttered by people with enough experience of hotel life to know better. Enthusiasm for design as a means in itself must be tempered. "Form follows function" is the opposing motto, which has been drummed into architecture and design since the beginning of the 20th Century, but which has remained a constant truth. Aesthetics do have a very real function, relating to balance

and harmony, and a structure's basic effect on the human senses. On the other side of the coin, functionality must also be considered an integral part of aesthetics, and blending these two elements is where skill is required. Design that rejects function is, at best, freestyle.

From this perspective, the growing demand for design hotels is anything but a product of the zeitgeist. Placing whatever is flashy or conspicuous into this bracket is to turn the philosophy of real design hotels on its head. Such hotels are no longer an exotic phenomenon, but a long-term development, an answer to a modern need for equilibrium and unity.

The hotels in this book have been chosen on this basis, but what makes them worthy of the label "best designed"? The most obvious common point is that they each have a recognizable, overall concept. Superficial styling is deception, and "overall" means a hotel

that is consistent, from furniture and fabrics to restaurant menu, with service that anticipates guests' wishes, and acts accordingly; not a celebration of fusty old habit. Prerequisites that are neither difficult nor expensive to realize. Millions of dollars are not necessarily called for, but what is crucial is a good idea and its accomplished realization. And a mellifluousness that attracts, relaxes and inspires.

If one examines hotels according to these criteria it will soon become apparent that there are still just as few as ever that fulfil them. The authors have researched a number of these exceptions, and collected the results in this book. As varied as the properties may be, so united are they by their charm, uniqueness and coherence.

The journey through nine countries – from Turkey to Great Britain, from Germany to Portugal – is a whistlestop tour of fascinating landscapes. And throughout these beautiful

09　　　　　　　　　　　　　**10**　　　　　　　　　　　　　**11**

locations, one comes across select, tasteful guesthouses, with extraordinary architecture and top design. Outstanding mountain hotels, such as the Aparthotel St. Anton in the Austrian Alps, with its glazed, roof-top sauna, where guests can purify body in the damp heat, while nourishing the soul with views across the Zwölfköpfer and Eisenspitze peaks. Or the Saratz in Pontresina, Switzerland. A noble property, breathed back into modern life, tingling with friendliness. Not just a contrast from its situation, but also its concept, is the Castelnau Des Fiumarcon, run by Frédéric Coustols; a collection of 17 affectionately restored houses in French Gascogne. Available to rent separately or as an entire village, the service may be minimal but the inspirational value is huge.

Architectural and culinary excellence is offered by France's masterchef, Michel Bras, at his restaurant and hotel in the L'Aubrac hills. The bravely futuristic architecture of his construction is an example of the lightness with which one can combine a roof over one's head and the surrounding nature.

A number of the hotels introduced in this book are also distinguished samples of old, sometimes historic substance fused with contemporary architectural techniques and concepts. The combination of "new" materials such as steel, glass and concrete within ancient walls can be well studied in the Portuguese pousadas. Consummate talent is shown in Eduordo Souto do Moura's reconstructed Pousada Santa Maria do Bouro, close to Braga, in the far north of Portugal. Casting off any kind of historicism, he has translated and driven the grace of the former Cistercian convent into our time. Antonio Esteva's fincas on Mallorca also display skilful choices of colour and material. These kinds of projects continue to lend weight to the maxim "less is more", removing unnecessary decoration to bring the natural hues, textures and forms of the original buildings to the forefront.

Wind, weather and water also play a central role at the coastal hotels presented here. Whether on the North German outcrop Helgoland, at the Alison Brooks designed Hotel Atoll, Olga Polizzi's Tresanton in the British county of Cornwall, or the Estalagem da Ponta do Sol on Madeira. One-hundred metres above the steep cliffs of the Portuguese island, the panorama swings from ocean to terraced hills, and from sub-tropical, lush green mountainsides to the slick, reserved architecture of Tiago Oliveira's complex. A composite of modesty, usefullness, art and intelligence. As with all the 40 design hotels in this book, it is a refuge for the discovery of beauty, and a specimen of the perfect counteraction between the natural and man-made.

A place of inspiration.

06 | Terrace at the Farol Design Hotel, Cascais, Portugal.

07 | Son Gener, Mallorca. Natural stone and ancient olive trees.

08 | Courtyard at Hotel San Roque, Tenerife.

09 | Sauna with Alpine views, at the Aparthotel St. Anton. Architecture by Wolfgang Pöschl.

10 | A field of rape near the village of Castelnau Des Fieumarcon, in Gascony, France.

11 | High above the Atlantic lies the swimming pool at Estalagem da Ponta do Sol, Madeira.

aparthotel anton | st. anton am arlberg . austria

DESIGN: Wolfgang Pöschl

01

02

01| Facade with sliding sun-shades.

02| A centrepoint is the spiral staircase with balloon lights.

03 | Sauna with views across the mountain panorama.

04 | Functionally furnished, the living and sleeping areas can be separated by a sliding door. Large windows and light colours create a bright space.

The Aparthotel Anton, opened at the end of 2000, offers a base for winter sports in architecture that does not steal the show from the breathtaking surrounding Alps. It sits on the spot which, until recently, was raced through by the Transalpine express railway. Relocating the station to the outskirts of St. Anton am Arlberg created an opportunity to build a completely new hotel in the centre of a traditional winter resort. The location could not be better for passionate skiers or mountain climbers - step out of the hotel door and straight into the lift. The Galzig lift travels up to dizzying heights of between 1300 and 2811 metres and covers the well-known Valluga skiing area.

Architect Wolfgang Pöschl, for whom this hotel project was a first, demonstrates the courage to be differerent in an environment where the "yodel look" still dominates. Cement, steel, glass and wood give his structure a contemporary appearance, although the larch wood shingles covering the façade pay homage to the Arlberger building tradition. The Anton is a feel-good hotel. Sand-coloured loom chairs in the lobby and soothing colours remove any hint of severity, though their combination with the matt-green slate floor at the same time dismisses any trace of superficial cosiness. Like a signal, the hotel's bright-red lift travels through the building, its glass dome projecting a feeling of soaring towards the sky.

The rooms are sparsely furnished with high-quality functional fittings made of alder wood. Living and sleeping areas can be separated with a sliding door, and the well-equipped kitchenettes are hidden behind mirrored doors. Particularly comfortable are the deep window niches with their upholstered padded covers and leather rolls, best suited to whiling away an afternoon with a book. To shut out the sun, a stainless-steel grid can be pulled along the façade as required.

Photography by the Vienesse artist Martin Eiter, which can be viewed all around the property, sets an unconventional tone. Eiter has alientated motifs from their immediate surroundings to such an extent that some of the pictures are more reminscent of a moonscape than a mountain summit.

Young, simple fare is served in the popular bistro. The encirling wooden terraces are perfect for sunbathing, or sleeping off lunch. The highlight for most guests, however, is the glazed roof-sauna. Here you can purify body whilst feeding the mind with wonderful views of the Zwölfköpfe and Eisenspitz, before snoozing on the roof terrace.

03   **04**

05

06

05 | The window banks are ideal to sit and read, or just think in peace.

06| Opaque glass divides the bathroom from bedroom, allowing daylight in.

saint james | bouliac . france
DESIGN: Jean Nouvel

01

Jean-Marie Amat got through eight different architects before he found in Jean Nouvel, French star of the architectural world, a congenial partner with whom to realise his visions. In other words, with whom to create a hotel to match his unconventional style of cooking. Amat, for his part, is regarded as one of the brightest stars in French cookery, even though he quite deliberately contravenes the traditional rules of haute cuisine. His "Poulet de Bresse", for example, is stuffed with a farci of little olives rather than with black truffles, something which many French cooks and critics regard as tantamount to sacrilege.

It is, in the eyes of some contemporaries at least, a similar picture with the hotel Jean Nouvel built for him in the late 1980's right in the middle of the vineyards, in the rural idyll of Bouliac. Even now it is considered a pioneering achievement in state-of-the-art hotel architecture. The various buildings, which accommodate 15 rooms and three suites, stand out provocatively in the countryside. The iron trellises, once used in local tobacco farming and which now line the hotel's façades, are an important design feature. That they are covered in layer after layer of rust is intentional, giving the surface a matt reddish sheen.

Many of Nouvel's later creative achievements in his highly praised building for the Cultural Centre in Lucerne are already apparent here. The contrast of the dark hallways with the glisteningly bright rooms, the intense play of light and shade. Nouvel also designed the furniture, having the beds built especially high to allow guests lying in bed to enjoy moonlit views of Bordeaux at night. The rooms have only the very finest quality technical equipment, from Bang & Olufsen stereo systems to the high-tech reading lamp, with a pinpoint beam so accurate that one person can read in perfect illumination, while their partner

slumbers undisturbed. Even the 25-metre, slender swimming pool with mysteriously black shimmering water bears Nouvel's unmistakable signature.

In addition to the gourmet Restaurant Saint-James, awarded 18 points out of 20 by the Gault Millau Guide, there is also the Brasserie Le Bistroy, serving mainly regional cuisine, and the Café de l'Espérance.

02   **03**

04 | Inside is open and airy; one can see Nouvel's influence throughout.

05| Lightness and transparence let nature come to the forefront.

06| All 15 rooms and three suites have fantastic views of the vineyards.

04 05

01 | The Saint James, spread through four buildings, was one of Jean Nouvel's first hotel design projects, constructed in 1989.

02 | Light and shadow play crucial roles in the interior.

03 | The steel façade is coloured with rust. The window sections can be raised from within the rooms by remote control.

06

castelnau des fieumarcon | lagarde . france

DESIGN: Frédéric Pierre Coustols

02 | Bedroom in the Maison Bartherote, situated at the bottom
end of the village's "Rue Principale".

Doing things by halves is not Frédéric Coustols' style. Since his childhood, the former finance expert looked on with melancholy as Lagarde, a tiny village in the heart of Gascony, fell into decay. Although not far from the idyllic Lectoure, Lagarde's fate was similar to that of many other, often quite magnificent rural estates. Foreshadowing the Pyrenees, this hilly area has always been agricultural, thanks largely to the mildness of its climate. Compared with the Loire region, little grandeur has been attracted to these parts. Nevertheless, an almost indeterminable number of castles, palaces and splendid country seats still bear testimony to an earlier feudal structure. Not that it helped. The migration from the land that began in 1945, at the end of the Second World War, wore down even this smart hamlet sitting in splendour along the edge of a

mountain ridge. Coustols was there when one inhabitant after the other moved away from the village until, in 1975, the last remaining resident packed up and left in resignation.

This disintegration of rural ways and cultural values was very hard for Coustol's to accept. Although he became an internationally successful cosmopolitan, he never lost touch with his French roots. The question was, what should he do to turn the tide? Quite simply, he did what others might perhaps dream of doing, only to shy away in horror when they realise what it will entail. He bought the whole village including 35 hectares of surrounding countryside. This was not a quick process – it took him four years to persuade the 99 remaining owners and their heirs to entrust to him the ruins that had belonged to their

01 | Simply charming: in the largest of the 17 houses there are two bedrooms, a
kitchen and a living room measuring around 50m².

04

03 | Nearly every room has a little touch of art in it.

04 | For Frédéric Coustols, the gradual renovation of this tiny village represents his life's work.

05 | The history of the settlement dates back to the 12th Century.

forefathers. In 1979, Coustols became sole owner of a village whose origins go right back to the 12th Century and which even belonged to the English crown for a while. For a long period, in fact, the village was under the control of the Marquis des Fieumarcon, hence its name, until the last of his family fled from the French Revolution. That in turn resulted in a "cell division" among the people, leading eventually to the 99 remaining proprietors with whom Coustols needed to negotiate.

Once Coustols had taken possession of the village, it was to take him a further twenty years to tackle the remaining issues and bring the buildings into a state of repair suitable for renting to holidaymakers. Today, Castelnau des Fieumarcon is anything but a hotel; rather, it is an extraordinary place for a holiday in a grandiose setting,

05

06

06 | Pleasing details, such as the wood and stone stairs in Maison Antonin, can be found around every corner.

as well as a veritable insider's tip for anyone looking for a special, unusual venue. It is the perfect setting for all kinds of functions, whether corporate events, seminars, family celebrations, weddings and presentations such as fashion shows, or private viewings of art exhibitions. A more vivid gallery is hardly possible to imagine. This village, with its unique ambience, has also hosted a European Summer Academy for up-and-coming musicians and a competition for poets.

In its heyday around 1640, there were 250 people living in Lagarde; now, in its present form, the village can offer 26 bedrooms in the 17 buildings that have been restored so far. "Depending on the type of event, we can accommodate up to 70 people on the site", says Coustols. He is reluctant to create a great deal more capacity

"because a certain exclusivity is what gives the place its charm", although further plans are ready and waiting. The former stable buildings, which at first sight look like a fortress, already accommodate a hall, 100 metres long and 25 metres wide, which is used as the dining room and for events. Another room of similar dimensions, also to be used for events, is still a ruin, awaiting to be woken from its long sleep. When the visionary, multi-talented Coustols, a fat cigar on his lips, describes his ideas for the swimming pool "with a view", complete with sauna and steam bath, you cannot fail to be captivated, and there will only be one desire on your mind: to come back again as soon as possible to see the new creation.

08

07 | Bedroom in the Maison Cadeilhan, one of the first on the village's main road.

08 | 09 Shower with wall-high glass door, which leads to a private inner courtyard.

10 | The stairway at Maison Pujol leads up to both bedrooms on the second floor.

07   **09**   **10**

11 | Decorative arrangements are simple and tasteful, such as here, at the entrance to Maison Le Cercle.

12 | 14 Dining table and window in Maison Antonin

13 | The owner is an art collector and music lover - in Maison Preissac guests will find an antique harpsichord.

15 | A mirror with traces of history in Maison Cadeilhan.

16 | 17 Little touches of authenticity.

michel bras | laguiole . france
DESIGN: Eric Raffy

While the heavenly herbed lamb, soft as butter, is melting on your tongue, it is possible to come into serious difficulties. It's not easy to avoid making unseemly groans of saisfaction, and where should one look? At the artistic creation of the master chef, at the fascinatingly harsh isolation of the L'Aubrac mountains, or at your neighbour's trés chic outfit? With just 70 seats, the gourmet restaurant and its attached hotel in the Auvergne is recommended in the "Guide Michelin" not just as worthy of a detour, but as a destination in itself, outright.

For people with a passion for good food and original architecture, a weekend in this refuge could constitute an emotional high point. A contrast is on offer: the sumptuousness of the menu is countered by the spartan design of the hotel's 15 rooms, spread out along two elongated barrack-like buildings. Their simplicity is almost a man-made expression of the rugged, surrounding contours of the Auvergne.

Spartan does not equate to insufficient, however, and those that cannot do without their creature comforts are well served. An almost acerbic style is favoured with the tables, wardrobes and bathroom fittings. What is made abundantly clear is that the local landscape is the real star here, and the real source of genius. Through the generous use of glass in the lobby, bar and restaurant area, the surrounding hills and mountains are immediately present in almost every point of the property. Sit in one of the comfortable stuffed lobby chairs and gaze languidly into the distance - you may find yourself asking why people always make such a fuss about views of the sea? The mountainous landscape brings out a meditative element in visitors, and the avant-garde purism of designer Eric Raffy provides an impressive container to capture this.

01

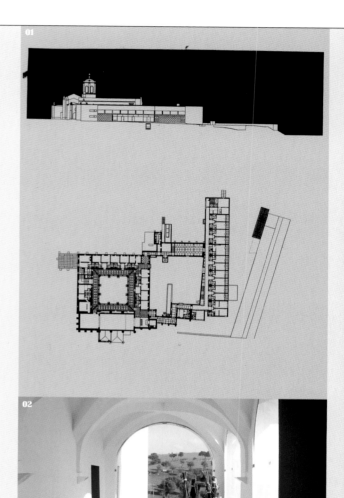

01

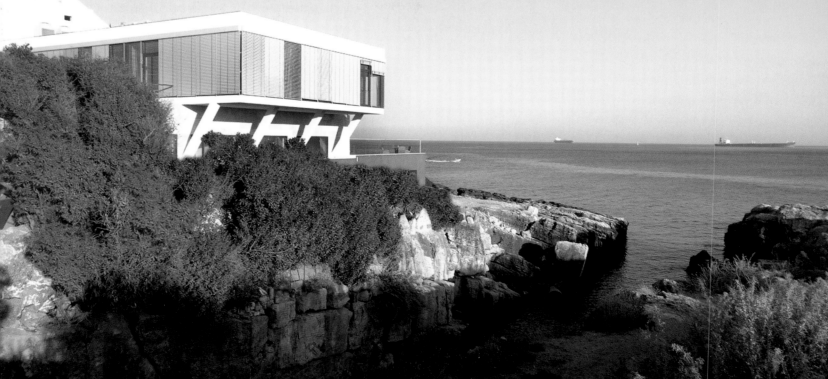

03 | 04 Wooden frameworks and glass characterize the architecture, reminiscent of traditional Japanese styles.

05 | A view of the heath from one of the rooms. The buildings are partially linked with roofed wooden walkways.

carducci 76 | cattolica . italy
DESIGN: Lucas Sgoi

01

02

Carducci 76, located on the outskirts of a notoriously famous roasting ground for over-sunned German tourists on the Adriatic coast, is the first luxury resort in Cattolica that caters for the design-crazy individualist. Alberta Ferretti is the name behind the clever, relaxed facelift of the 1920's villa. She is the head of Aeffe, the fashion imperium whose labels include those of designers like Jean-Paul Gaultier and Moschino. Her brother, Massimo, is the brain behind the gastronomic aspect of the family business and, together with the architect and designer, Lucas Sgoi, has completely

remodeled the property, restyling it into one of Italy's most renowned holiday locations.

Sitting on the terrace enjoying the fresh sea breeze, time passes by at an agreeably gentle rate. Alternatively, for those preferring more strenuous activities to perfecting the art of doing nothing gracefully, the ocean is only a couple of steps away, with its enticing water sports and sandy beach. Just in case the sun doesn't cooperate, guests can splash around just as nicely in the heated swimming pool, and also top up their tans in the solarium, where they can

retire after a round of fitness activities including cycling, rowing or jogging. A stint in the fitness area always saps one's energy, but the "Vicolo Santa Lucia" offers an ideal solution to regaining it. On balmy summer nights its delicious dishes are served under the stars, with the roar of the ocean and the rustle of swaying bamboo plants putting even the most die-hard city types into a more Italian state of mind. Those considering themselves too young for bed as the night wears on can take a 15-minute taxi ride to the "Cocorico" in Riccione, one of Italy's most renowned

03

01 | A villa from the 1920's is the home for this unusual Adriatic hotel..

02 | "Great Gatsby" elegance with a dash of Japanese minimalism.

03 | Guests who would rather avoid the beautiful but lively beach will find an oasis of peace at the hotel's pool.

35

04 | Modern Japanese styles, Islamic elements and typical Italian energy all combine at Carducci 76. With 38 rooms and four suites, the hotel has a personal atmosphere

05 | Restaurant "Vicolo Santa Lucia".

nightclubs.
On their return, breakfast can be enjoyed in "La Terrazza sul Giardino", on the garden terrace. This small, fine hotel restaurant serves light snacks all day long, as well as the only sushi to be found for miles around.

The 38 double rooms and three suites also project a simple elegance. The designers placed great emphasis on reviving the atmosphere of the decadent, charming '20's in this villa, and had no problems succeeding. The hotel is chilled-out and light. Round arches, soft upholstered furniture and wooden tables complete the picture in the rooms. Modern elements are combined with Japanese living culture and Islamic flavours, mingled with the typical flair of Italy's coast. The balance is partly achieved, and certainly enhanced, through Yin-Yang effects – white marble, black leather, zebra and tiger print decorative covers and paintings by Konnellis and Calzolari. Carducci 76 is also a fine base from which to quench a thirst for cultural knowledge, richly distributed throughout the picturesque regions around Urbino and Gradara. It is no surprise that the Ferretti family often entertain personalities including Jean-Paul Gaultier, Narciso Rodriguez and Rifat Ozbek. Creative minds always draw inspiration from extraordinary places.

villa fontelunga | arezzo . italy

DESIGN: Philipp Robinson

Blue sky, sunshine and a fresh breeze – it's not often that you get bad weather in Tuscany. Grounds enough then, to pack your bags and jet off. If you really need another reason, there is also Villa Fontelunga, nestled in picturesque olive groves near Arezzo. Since welcoming its first guests in June 2000, the doors to this calming, 19th-century country house have been open each year from March to November. A protected, private oasis, and the perfect place to enjoy the Italian Dolce Vita. Far away from the chaos of the city, the villa offers just nine rooms over three floors. Away from speeding traffic, stressed-out crowds and packed pavements, relax in the fresh, aromatic air.

Simon Carey and Philip Robinson, both Englishmen, and Paolo Kastener, Italian, have fulfiled a long-standing dream in this cozy hotel. In Villa Fontelunga, the three friends unite their typical national qualities. Paolo, with his latin temperament, ensures a lively atmosphere behind the property's stone walls, while Simon and Phillip create order and efficiency in their treasured house.

A mixture of traditional Tuscan lifestyle and contemporary design is on show throughout the building. Modern and antique furniture decorates the large rooms. It's easy just to sit in the villa and watch, listen, do nothing. Most guests, however, are drawn outside by the

01 | 02

01 | Swimming among the hills of Tuscany. The pool is surrounded by olive trees.

02 | There is no restaurant, but breakfast on the terrace can sometimes take all morning. The hosts sometimes cook for guests - always to Mama's recipe.

splendid landscape that wraps itself around the hotel. After a swim in the 15-metre pool surrounded by olive trees, sprawl out on warmed sun-lounger, book in hand, and dry in the tingly rays of summer. Even the gently chirping sparrows sound chilled-out.

Breakfast is always served on the terrace, accompanied by conversation with the owners. There is no restaurant at the hotel itself, but its environment is full of small cafés, bars, trattorias and eateries serving typical, local food. Horse-riding and golf can also be arranged, and sight-seeing couldn't be easier, with Florence just one hour away by car.

Whether a visit to a museum, a concert, the vineyards of Montepulciano or the nearby outlet stores for Prada, Dolce & Gabbana and Fendi, Simon, Phillip and Paolo will be on hand to advise and guide guests in the right direction. If they don't know what's cool in the sun, then who does?

03 | The 19th Century mansion affords a taste of the Dolce Vita.

04 | A balanced mixture of antique and modern furniture graces the spacious rooms.

pousada dom afonso II | alcácer do sal . portugal
DESIGN: Diogo Pimentel

01 | Pool and new wing.

In Alcácer do Sal, around 75km from the capital city Lisbon, lies the Pousada Dom Afonso II, on the main route between Setubal and the Algarve. The town and the castle in which the hotel is located, sit elevated above a wide, green valley, with the River Sado flowing at its base. The fertile plain is used today, as it has been for many years, for the farming of rice and pine trees.

Both city and fortress share a long human history, tracing back to the Neolithic period. One after another, raiders and conquerors left their own tracks, with fragments and clues still visible today. Renowned as a port since the 6th Century B.C., the Phoenician settlement was captured by the Romans, who made the location into a central trading point for goods from North Africa and the East. Business and commerce blossomed, and defences (castrum) were built, together with forums and basilicas.

In the 8th Century, the Moors seized the town, and created their own stronghold. The Vikings followed for a short while, but it was not until 1217 that Alcacer do Sal became Portuguese, under King Afonso II. Some 300 years later, the castle had already lost its military purpose, and was converted into a convent for Carmelite nuns. This religious group reached their most productive period in the 17th Century, culminating in the construction of a new convent building complete with church.

It is through the convent gate that hotel guests enter the complex, stepping straight into a stately, dignified atmosphere. Arched walkways, alive with a play between light and shadow, give an immediate hint to the unusual hotel experience that guests can expect. As contrast to the vast, monumental walls, the 35 rooms, including two suites, are minimalist and modern.

Rather than "historisize" the pousada, Diogo Pimentel has employed natural colours, fabrics and components to fashion a warm ambience. Simple designer furniture stands alongside antique, in a mutually complementary co-existence. Outside, the gardens extend the secluded-yet-open feel, with herbs and olive trees perfuming the breeze. Oaks stretch into the sky, and the valley below extends to a distant horizon.

03

02 | 75 km from Lisbon, the fort gained its name from King Dom Afonso II, who liberated the neighbouring Alcacer do Sal in 1217.

03 | The large reception hall.

04 | A cloister from the 17th Century, when the complex was used as a convent for the Carmelite order .

pousade st. maria do bouro | amares . portugal

DESIGN: Eduardo Souto de Moura

There was nothing left of this former monastery, near the town of Braga in Portugal's extreme northwest, before architect Eduardo Souto de Moura won a competition to rebuild and transform it into a pousada. The architect's winning plan for the building, which was originally founded by the Cistercian order in 1162, was based on the retention of as much of its original structural integrity as possible, while providing the necessary infrastructure for a modern hotel.

Today, the pousada's 33 somewhat spartan rooms are reminiscent of a modern take on a monk's cell. A visit to the Pousada Santa Maria do Bouro is surely as close as one can get to monastical life in contemplative comfort.

The pousada, however, is not just ideal for solitude seeking.

It also offers a perfect setting for corporate gatherings. These may be centred around the former kitchen, which is today the "eating and conversation hall". The careful handling of old materials and the care taken during the new construction is striking, leaving a contemporary edge. Examples include the partial replacement of old support beams with steel girders, and the introduction of additional light into the pousada's interior s.

These interventions are never a distraction, but actually support the historical character of the property by highlighting new construction and materials. It's a process which has been undertaken at the pousada in accordance with modern demands, and the resulting hotel is a vibrant space where the ghosts of the past blend with the spirit of the future.

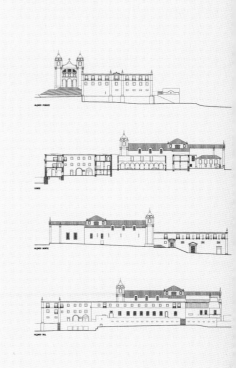

01

02

03

01 | Part of an old cloister.

04

02 | Projections of the pousada from all four sides.

03 | External view of the property. Behind the wall is the swimming pool.

04 | Internal courtyard.

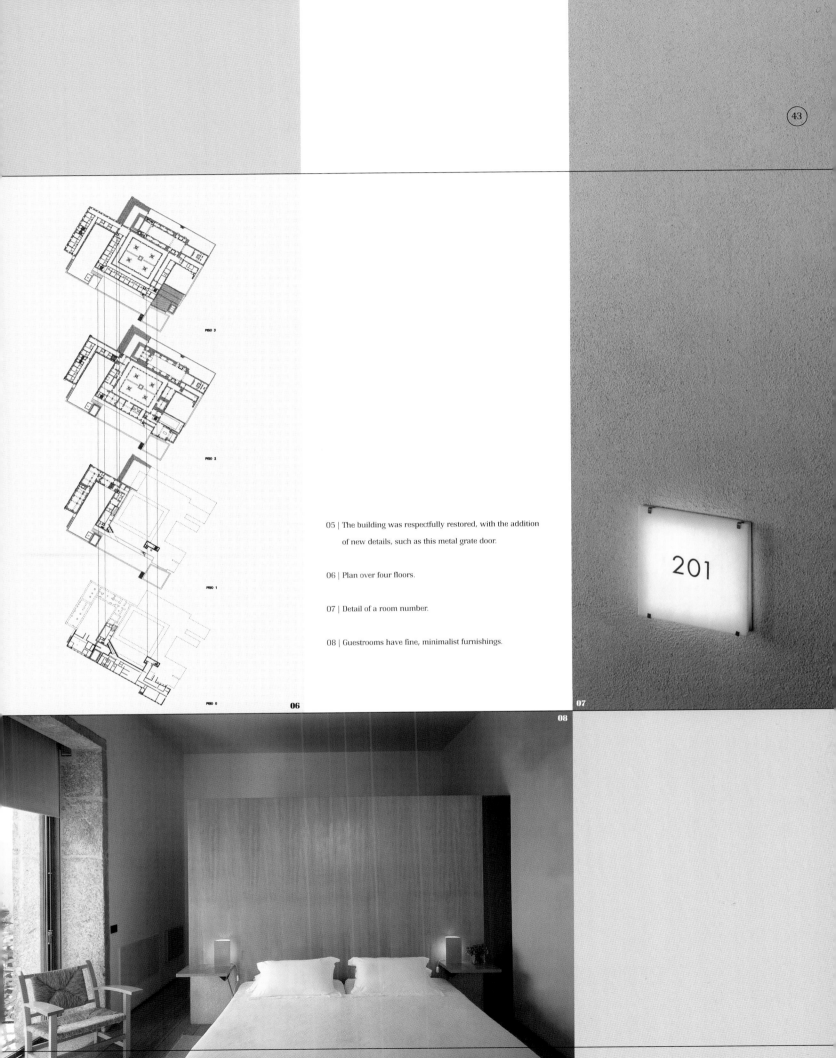

05 | The building was respectfully restored, with the addition
of new details, such as this metal grate door.

06 | Plan over four floors.

07 | Detail of a room number.

08 | Guestrooms have fine, minimalist furnishings.

pousada de nossa senhora da assunçao | arraiolos . portugal

DESIGN : Jose Paolo dos Santos, Christina Guedes

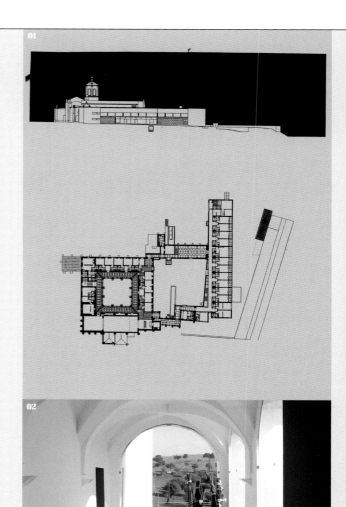

The foundation for the Pousada de Nossa Senhora da Assunçao was laid in 1496, when the convent was owned by Afonso Garcês, secretary to the three kings of the Portuguese territory, Afonso V, Joao II and Manuel. His son inherited the property on Garcês' death, and in turn donated it to the charitable Order of St. Eloi. In 1527, this religious order proceeded to develop the structure and adjoining small estate into a hospital and farm, renovating in the Manuelian and Rennaissance styles that were fashionable at the time, with the works finally completed in 1575. The complex carried out its charitable and Christian functions upto 1834, when the religious orders were disbanded, and the property was sold into private hands.

Over the decades that followed, the cloister's exterior and interior fell into a bad state of disrepair. The pousada programme proved to be a second chance for the neglected construction, and remodelling began in the early 1990's with Jose Paolo dos Santos restoring the damaged façade and roof using new materials and concrete. The interiors were kept as untouched a possible, allowing the property's pre-existing spatial qualities to be preserved and incorporated into the new structure. An autonomous new wing was also built to house guestrooms and other hotel work areas. It has an unashamedly modern design, which adds further power to the original cloister's historical substance and authenticity.

The pousada's interior architecture by Christina Guedes is simple, bright and makes use of mainly natural colours, such as white, beiges and brown tones. Guestrooms are sparsely furnished, with wooden floors creating a warm effect, while leaving the temperature cool, protecting visitors from the baking sun of the Alentejo landscape.

01 | Partial view of the new wing where the restaurant is located.

02 | Side projection of the new building and ground plan of the entire complex. To the left is the old convent with cloister, to the right, the new section.

03 | Part of the cloister, with entrances to the rooms in the old section of the pousada.

04 | New wing with guestrooms. In the
   foreground, a section of the long
   swimming pool.

05 | View into the modern courtyard, linking the
   old cloister with the contemporary block.

04

05

06

07

06 | Stone and wood are prevalent in the bathrooms.

07 | Finely crafted and sleek, the furnishings reflect a modern
interpretation of monastical life.

08 | Some rooms come complete with open fireplace.

farol design hotel | cascais . portugal

DESIGN: CM Dias Arquitectos LDA

Lisbon International Airport, estimated time of arrival: 20:00. In a taxi, one drives the nearly 25 kilometres, always west, always towards the sea, to Cascais… and what did it say in the travel guide? "The Estoril coast is well known for its comfortable climate and fine, white, sandy beaches. Lush, green landscapes with pine trees stretch up into the Sintra mountains…". The breathtaking sunset quite literally puts all of this in the shade. Looking back, the red-gold light makes the countryside appear softly drawn in pastels. The more the last rays of the sun turn the horizon violet, the closer the lights of the palatial villa on the cliffs

become. With a salted beeze wafting through the taxi's open window, it's time to lay back and dream.

Suddenly one finds oneself in the bustle of Cascais' narrow alleys, in one of the most expensive residential areas around Lisbon. The taxi driver, who has by now also become tour guide and promoter, tells of the farmers' and fishermen's markets that take place in the historic centre of the town. Skilfully, he negotiates the yacht marina and you are finally there: the Farol Design Hotel.

The first thing that one notices is the situation, perched on

rocks in the middle of a foaming Atlantic Ocean, bordered on 180 degrees by water. Directly next door lies the old Guia lighthouse, earlier versions of which guided seafarers around the perilous cliffs back in the Middle Ages. The heart of the hotel beats in a villa from 1890, that was once in the ownership of the Duke of Cabral. In 2002, the building was completely renovated, and furnished with a new infrastructure, which now houses lobby, restaurant and bar.

The majority of the 31 guestrooms and three suites, as well as both conference rooms, are located in a new wing. With its straight lines and geometric structure,

01

02

03

01 | The new block housing guestrooms sits directly over the cliffs.

02 | A view from one of the balconies to the large wooden terrace on the ground floor.

03 | Panorama of the Bay of Cascais, one of the most popular leisure destinations in western Portugal.

04

05

06

this section is not just the aesthetic high-point of the complex, but also offers a kind of natural "open living". The rooms, all with parquet floors, wooden terraces or marble balconies, can be summed up in three words: wood, light and water. Thanks to the room-high glazing, the junction between internal and external is completely transparent. The clear forms of the white-brown minimalist furniture in combination with the sound of the sea, almost close enough to touch, make a wonderful nest in which to recharge your creative batteries.

During the daytime, the open-ended panorama of the ocean makes a mesmerizing stage, whatever the weather. Working in this fruitful environment is a pleasure, whether on developing a concept, writing a text or brainstorming with a team. If pure holiday is all that's likely to occupy your thoughts, delights can also be found in the form of the hotel restaurant's gastronomic palette, or in the myriad of golden beaches that speckle the coast.

04 - 06 | With 31 rooms and three suites, the Farol Design Hotel has an intimate size.

07 | The hotel's refreshing swimming pool.

08 | The property sits next door to this lighthouse.

09 | Open living.

pousada flor da rosa | crato . portugal

DESIGN: Jose Carrilho da Graca

01

The pousada "Flor da Rosa" is one of nine fortress complexes in the Mamede region, not far from the Spanish border, all joined together by a circular linking road. The hotel owes its magnificent name to a legend from the Middle Ages: A wounded knight, with only days to live, received a rose from his lover, as a sign of her fidelity and bond to him, to accompany the knight on his last journey. Fate intervened, however, and as the knight became healthy again, his maiden died before him. He was inconsolable, and ordered that the castle should be named "Flor da Rosa", in memory of his lost love, before dying himself, of a broken heart.

Today, the fortress complex close to Crato is a successful example of how historical substance can be blended with innovative architecture. Cut-stone walls, metres thick; filigree battlements, oriels, cloisters and a picturesque bell tower all find optical harmony with steel girders, concrete surfaces and laminated glass. Carrilho da Graca set himself the goal of preserving the original, ancient charisma of the convent, but set off in contrast with modern-day elements. Gaudy over-decoration would be just as gruesome for the designer as it would be for the majority of the pousada's guests.

The construction, with its impressive, massive walls, built for defence, can look back at a long and varied past. A religious centre since time immemorial, Crato was given over to the Knights Templar after its re-conquest by the Portugese under King Sancho II. These knights, an order with a military bias, were to defend the area towards the south and the

02

03

01 | The old walls of the hotel originate from the 12th Century, when the fortress was built by the order of the Temple Knights.

02 | Lounge and bar in the vaulted hall, where the order would hold meetings.

03 | This stairway illustrates how harmonious the combination of ancient stone and modern furniture can be…

neighbouring plateau. In 1356, the convent and fortified palace were built two kilometres outside the town walls.

Through the transformation of rooms that were earlier of importance, but became increasingly redundant, da Graca attempted to intensify the visual and physical experience that the building offers, with a clear departure from museum-styled conservation. The imposing cloister has been integrated into the hotel hall. Heavy curtains, endless collections of medieval weapons and armour, and huge, dark oil paintings have been replaced by the aesthetic of pure materials, making the interior's lines and forms even more splendid and inspiring. The lobby and bar are among the most impressive areas, where noble seating and subtle lighting have created an elegant, refined atmosphere in the vaulted hall. The same is true of all 23 rooms, three of which are in the pousada's tower. Airy, light and, above all, large, they combine comtemporary colours and textures, bringing new energy to an ancient place.

pousada flor da rosa | crato . portugal

06

05

07

04| …as do the historic building's 11 guestrooms.

05 | The restaurant serves regional dishes.

06 | A further 13 rooms can be found in the new
building.

07 | The complex also has a sheltered swimming
pool.

choupana hills resort & spa | madeira . portugal

DESIGN: Michel de Camaret, Didier Lefort

01

02

03

Those accustomed to flat countryside and straight roads would be advised to either let themselves be chauffered around or to start off gently by climbing the less daunting hills. Even powerful cars can only manage certain ascents in first gear, and the descents require very reliable brakes. Funchal's streets, or alleyways to be exact, easily put those of San Francisco in the shade and promise a thrilling, white-knuckle experience. To reach Madeira's newest luxury resort, such test rides can be enjoyed to the full. Up high, still a way above the already imposing, famous botanical gardens, on a completely exposed plateau and in the midst of lush, sub-tropical vegetation, investors have built a new style resort and wellness hotel, with 34 elegantly designed houses perched on stilts.

Early in the planning stage, the group of architects, Frenchmen Michel de Camaret and Didier Lefort, drew up an ecological concept that would entail integrating the surrounding nature as a fundamental component. The wood used for fixtures and furniture originates from Asia. Its use is balanced out by an extensive forestry programme for the tropical rain forest.

At the heart of the resort is an extensive range of health, beauty and wellness offers, with massage techniques from around the globe, including hydromassages. Aromatherapy is also available, as are revitalising baths, sauna, Turkish hammam, face and body treatments, as well as diets or set nutrition plans. The architecture and design

take on a significant meaning, in the knowledge that the aesthetic surroundings promote a sense of well-being and enhance stimulation.

The buildings, internal areas, furniture, decoration and plants are interwoven with the external areas such as pathways, garden, swimming pool or terraces. The harmonious architecture reveals a depth of feeling, and mixes all kinds of elements from the history of Portuguese art with Asian forms and contemporary internationalism. Tropical woods and coconut mats, for example, are juxtaposed with fine linen cloth and smooth, uniformly painted walls. Buddha statues stand alongside futuristically elegant bars and steel/wood constructions; Tibetan antiques share space with contemporary seating interpretations and bar stools.

04

05

06

01 | In the newest luxury resort on Madeira, guests can find refuge among sub-tropical nature.

02 - 04 | All rooms have a living and sleeping area with bathroom, and a huge terrace.

05 | In the evening sunshine, the terrace railings cast interesting shadows. The suites each have a jacuzzi tub sunk into the terrace floor.

06 | View across Funchal to the ocean

07

08

09

10

07 | Individual design rules, through to the smallest
     detail, such on as the wardrobe doors...

08 | ...or on the sliding door between bedroom and
     bathroom.

09 | Bar and lounge on the top floor. Below, the Xopana
     restaurant serves fusion cuisine.

10 | View across the pool to the wellness centre in one of
     the two main buildings.

Almost all of the furniture is designed by Didier Lefort. His signature already marks the furnishings of the Datai on the Malaysian island of Langkawi. Except for the four suites, all the villas on wooden stilts — referred to as bungalows — are divided into two 40m² units with living and sleeping quarters, an airy bathroom flooded with natural daylight, as well as an extensive terrace made of wooden boards. Two full-length sliding glass doors can be fully opened and form a seamless link between the internal area and the terrace, which covers an area of almost 30m². From here the panoramic view over Funchal towards the ocean lying far below is sensational. This view can also be enjoyed from the main buildings, drawing on fine Asian architecture, with their reception, lobby, various terraces, wellness centre with indoor pool, bar and restaurant. Those swimming a few lengths in the green shimmering lagoon-pool will undoubtedly keep pausing, namely whenever they take in the view of the blue ocean, merging visually with the flat edge of the overflowing water.

11 | A mixture of Asian purism and regional influences determine the design of the property.

12 | Terrace above the wellness centre.

crowne plaza resort | madeira . portugal

DESIGN: Ricardo Nogueira, Duarte Caldeira Silva

A pair of cheerily nattering white bathrobes walk down the long, cool corridor, and enter the lift at its end. The press of a button, a short wait, the doors open – the bathrobes move forward into the cabin. Almost like peering out from a lighthouse, the rear glass wall affords a spectacular view of the ocean. Out on the shorefront, the couple make their way to the two huge, deep-blue saltwater pools, and prepare themselves for the first, exciting exploratory plunge.

The remarkable volume of these strictly geometrically laid out pools, bare of any adornment, is indicative of the size of the resort, and its organisation as a wellness and conference hotel. With 300 rooms and suites, it is the newest major project on Madeira in the five-star segment and is not typically representative of the other, mostly smaller, buildings presented in this book. The concept, however, is certainly interesting. The private investor and owner, an established lover of art and architecture, commissioned two of his fellow countrymen, Ricardo Nogueira and Duarte Caldeira Silva, to plan both the complex and his private house, situated immediately beside it.

Even when driving by, along the "Estrada Monumental" coastal road – the name of the road is perfectly apt – the colossus towers up in the foreground. In contrast to other large hotels, the modernity and transparency of the construction is immediately striking, created, to an extent, by extensive glazing. The two identically arranged halves of the building form an open, bright effect, a seemingly appropriate response to the concrete blocks and almost criminally bad architecture of

01

02

bygone days. Optically, the façade is particularly attractive at dusk when the interior is lit. The blue colour of the corridor walls on all 10 floors radiates through the glass fronts, bathing the façade in an eerily atmospheric glow.

While the rooms are practical and promise a comfortable stay, complete with Philippe Starck furnished balconies and sea views, they appear rather

less innovative compared with the hotel's architecture and the design of the internal public areas. They are reminiscent of American luxury chains which, although not to be sneered at in the hotel business as a whole, seldom produce original results. The rooms would certainly have benefited from the use of lighter materials, more minimalism and more daylight – especially in the bathrooms. That said, the

01 | In the atrium.

02 | Functional details, such as these ventilation chutes, have also been made decorative.

03 | Illuminated view of the hotel from the Estrada Monumental.

04 | Glass is the dominant building material in this new grand hotel.

05 | View from the 10th floor towards the foyer.

06 | The breakfast bistro. Almost the same amount of tables are situated in the open air.

property's "Crowne Plaza Resort" label is somewhat misleading in a positive sense, projecting an image not quite congruent with its uncommon architectonic concept and service standards.

The interior design of the breakfast hall and lobby remains compelling, situated in the right and left wings of the building, beneath the entrance area, in a museum-like atrium spread over three floors. Intensified by the brightness of the glass fronts, these areas appear very airy and give the impression of sitting in an enormous outdoor covered art gallery – especially as the doors to the terraces, situated in front, are mostly wide open. Immediately next to this are the two main restaurants; the more exclusive "Wild Orchid" with its fusion cuisine and "La Brasserie" with its light French cuisine. Those preferring fresh fish can eat in the simpler "Cervejara Portuguesa" on the pool deck.

The main attraction is most certainly the huge spectrum of wellness treatments on offer at the "Marine Spa", including a complete range of thalasso therapy. More standard facilities include the sauna, steam baths and indoor pool. Features such as the two squash courts, the kids club and the hotel's own diving platform, are certainly worth a special mention. With its striking architecture and impressive guest portfolio, the resort is a contemporary, modernist answer to the traditional grand hotel.

07 **08**

09

10

11

12

07 | The hotel's two enormous saltwater pools are unique for the island.

08 | One of the lounges, with the ocean always in sight.

09 | Side table in the secomd lounge.

10| Presidential suite on the 10th floor.

11 | 12 Living room in the Presidential suite.
The hotel's other rooms are spacious, but not especially innovative.

estalagem da ponta do sol | madeira . portugal

DESIGN: Tiago Oliveira

If the water was just a couple of degrees warmer, swimmers would probably emerge with wrinkled fingers and toes, as if from a long, leisurely bath. The swimming pool counts among those places at Estalagem da Ponta do Sol where one could stay forever, gazing out in fascination. Luckily, the temperature is cool enough that, after a few laps, returning to a warm sun lounger doesn't seem like an altogether bad idea.

A good 100 metres above steep cliffs, the view swings along a rocky coast, over the ocean, terraced hills and green, subtropical mountains, before coming to chic, reserved architecture. The complex, by the young Portugese architect, Tiago Oliveira, unifies all the aesthetic, care, usefulness, poetry and intelligence that one often wishes from architecture, but seldom experiences. This recent member of the "design hotels" group is a place for the discovery of beauty, and is well-suited to a study of the harmonious bond between nature and architecture.

The drive from the airport takes around 45 minutes; from Funchal it's around 30. The motorway leads through tunnels and over bridges, and finally along the stony shoreline. In the distance, the new construction crowns a projecting cliff with a beam of white. One last tunnel, a roundabout, and the vista suddenly changes. A bridge is the optical centrepoint, high up, linking the new building to the lift tower of the main structure – an old "Quinta", a Portugese estate, with living quarters once belonging to the local lord.

01 | A throne above the Atlantic.

02 | The hotel restaurant sits on an outcrop of rock, and offers a spectacular view of the ocean, the village of Ponta do Sol below and the hills opposite, filled with banana plantations.

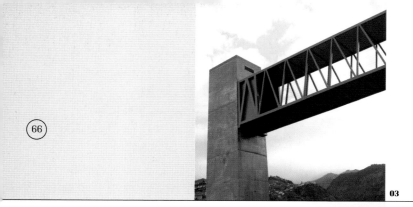

03

04

A more spectacular location is difficult to imagine. All of the hotel's sections divide themselves along slate outcrops that tumble down to the sea. The two-storey main building, with reception, lobby, bar and clubroom, stands elevated above Ponta do Sol, encompassed by a roofed terrace and gardens with ancient trees and palms. Sinking into one of the wicker chairs, drinking a café com leite and enjoying the panorama of blue on blue – that's true luxury.

One floor, or better said, one layer of rock further up, Tiago Oliveira has placed an aesthetic highlight: the restaurant. The cuisine may be simple, almost rustic, but the setting is grandiose. A backdrop of surf, boulders, lush vegetation over rolling mountains and a fishing village that looks like it's been painted in oils. The edifice itself is a simple, white cube, glazed from floor to ceiling, with an introverted interior design.

Its geometric clarity and renunciation of decorative elements makes guests' appreciation of the natural environment, as well as the architecture, somehow more intense.

From the restaurant, a series of steps (or, less strenuously, a lift and bridge) leads to the 54 guestrooms, characterised by their predominantly white walls and reduced furnishing. Everything is kept to a minimum, but everything is there. The corridors run like bowed arcades, open to the air. Strolling down these elegant walkways, it is perfectly usual to see guests wander direct from their rooms to the pool, clad simply in slippers and a bath robe. All rooms have their own balcony or terrace, and those facing west have views across the village, hills and ocean. These rooms are also slightly larger than those that sit directly over the cliffs, towards the east.

03 | The lift leads from the lobby and club rooms…

04 | 05 … to the connected bridge, high in the air.

05

06 | View towards the restaurant from the bridge.
Steps and walkways also connect the buildings.

07 | In the building to the right, behind the pool, are
the so-called Cliff Rooms.

08 | The rooms are located in two separate buildings.
They all have some form of sea-view.

09 | 10 The newly built bistro terrace affords an
incomparable panoramic view.

11 | A laid-back atmosphere, uncomplicated service and civil prices make the hotel a closely guarded tip for lovers of originality.

12 | Nothing is too much, but nothing is missing. The reserved interior design allows nature in.

13 | View across the pool's edge to the Atlantic. Thanks to the Gulf Stream, the island enjoys a constant, comfortable climate.

The easterly rooms are clearly more popular, however, as they are also the most expensive; even though at Estalagem da Ponta do Sol, one cannot really talk about "expensive". With prices starting at around 100 Euro a night, the hotel counts among those secret tips that definitely offer extraordinary value for money.

There's no way to consider the Estalagem, other than as aconcentrated charge of fascination, a real discovery – an almost unknown place of relaxation, revelation and inspiration. New pictures are formed every other moment, in the changing of the sunlight and the outlines of the clouds. The meditative, penetrating cymbal crash of waves on the battered coast becomes a mantra, and all guests long to do is watch and listen, trying to catch the faint, fresh taste of sea salt on their tongue.

14 | A part of the wellness area with fitness room, sauna, jacuzzi and small indoor pool.

16 | In the background is the entrance to the bistro and wellness area.

15 | The waves break on the rocks, 100 metres below the balcony.

17 | Tiago Olivera has created an example of how architecture and nature can be seamlessly joined.

quinta da casa branca | madeira . portugal

DESIGN: João Favila V.S. Menezes, Teresa Gois Ferriera, Luís Rosário

Funchal is an extremely peaceful town. Stretching from the rocky Atlantic coast over the small freight and cruise-liner harbour, over a mass of rolling hills and steep rock formations, it winds upwards between concrete and parks into the mountainous landscape with its subtropical vegetation. Though the area is heavily developed, slightly reminiscent of the Italian and French Riveria, the town, rather than being spoilt by this, has retained its idyllic appearance. With around 130,000 inhabitants and a great deal more tourists, Funchal may no longer be a village, but nor is it loud or hectic.

The small municipality has a truly urban and international flair, due perhaps also to the fact that the island's government continues to decide its own fate autonomous of its motherland, Portugal. There is a club and bar scene, though relatively limited. Most tourists belong to the more advanced age groups.

Aside from the warm climate, another important aspect for the high standard of living in Funchal are the many green areas within the town itself. The town is a jumbled mix of close-ranked buildings, parks, copses, ravines, rock faces too steep to

be built on, bare fields and huge private properties. Many of these were once managed estates, often banana plantations, in the hands of large Portugese or British landowners. The tourist boom was responsible for the bananas disappearing from the centre and outskirts of Funchal to make room for more hotels and guesthouses.

The Quinta da Casa Branca shares a similar history. The five-star property lies well hidden on a hill overlooking the ocean, in the middle of a vibrantly colourful park a mere 200 metres

or so above the legendary 150-year-old Reid's Palace and roughly a 20-minute walk from the harbour and town centre. The property is well disguised, its hidden driveway is reminiscent of the entrance to a grand villa. Behind the wrought-iron gate, however, is not the palatial building one would expect to see, but a dazzling filigreed glass house; a strictly geometric cube. The building won João Favila Menezes and his partner Maderia's most important architectural prize in 1999. One of the most impressive areas that shows the design to its best advantage, especially at dusk, is

04

01 | The hotel has a surprisingly central location in Funchal.

02 | Façade of the newly created bistro, serving breakfast, lunch and snacks. The other building offers a gourmet restaurant.

03 | Cool, but warmly-coloured corridors are an escape fom the summer heat

05　　　　　　　　　　　　　　**06**

04 - 06 | The reception is an architectural highlight, with a panorama of Funchal and the Atlantic Ocean. It reminds one of Mies van der Rohe's Barcelona Pavillion, but connects with the surrounding nature more effectively.

the terrace to the rear of the reception area, which affords a direct view of the ocean over the hills of the town, the hotel park and the noble private villas.

The 43 guest rooms, 12 superior and two suites, are located beneath the reception pavillion, with direct access to the garden, and in a further twostorey building, which was completed early in 2002. This structure also houses a limited wellness centre offering sauna, steam bath, fitness, jacuzzi and massage facilities. A charming peculiarity is the family Rolls Royce from the 1940's, which is used, complete with chauffeur, for ferrying guests around the local area.

The history of the property dates back to the mid 19th Century when the Scottish ancestors of the current owners, the Leacock family, cultivated wine and bananas on the land, then still covering an area of six hectares. The hotel, situated directly next to their house, still offers its guests roughly two hectares of open green space with exotic plants, a well-heated pool, breakfast pavilion and a gourmet restaurant in one of the oldest buildings on the land.

It was the owner's openness and curiosity, together with his faith in the capability of the architects, who were friends of the family, that made the

07

08

07 | Behind the reception is a small covered terrace – perfect for afternoon tea.

08 | 09 Quinta da Casa Branca is in a two-hectare park, home to a multitude of trees that are centuries old.

creation of this little jewel possible. It also led to a true architectonic rarity being created step-by-step from the initial mish-mash of styles in the interior design and garden furnishings; a process that is still ongoing. João Favila Menezes convinced his client with cool reason and clear sense: "My aim was to allow the powerful beauty of the natural environment to take effect using subdued, transparent architecture. This was also the reason we primarily used glass and black stone."

The guests mostly still fit the Madeira cliché: distinguished, conservative and greying. With the combination of contemporary architecture and a young, fresh service concept, the still-young French-Portuguese director, Isabel F. Ferraz, is aiming towards an integrative change of generations: "Casa Branca is, after all, the hottest place on the island…," she says with a wink, adding "…as far as the weather's concerned, anyway."

ocean drive | ibiza . spain

DESIGN: Anke Rice, Semi Masso

01

Ibiza – Island of the rich and beautiful, embodiment of the easy life. A place where the days glide by, and the nights are made to party, the booming techno and house beats emanate in restless rhythm from the clubs. A distinctly Mediterranean version of a global phenomenon. A lifestyle drunk on amusement, unreservedly dedicated to worldly pleasures, seeing and being seen. In this sphere, style is on a par with personality, and the hotel one chooses is just as important as the shoes one wears.

Directly on the chic "Botafoch" marina, and just a few minutes from the sandy Talamanca Bay, Ocean Drive Hotel offers this lifestyle clique suitable quarters. The entrance and lobby make a first and lasting impression of the property's simple sophistication, filled with smoothly polished marble and classic furniture. Le Corbusier's seating cubes and sofas make an appearance, as do Mies van de Rohe's Barcelona chairs. In keeping, the restaurant presents itself as a slick Italian outfit, serving delicious, southern

European food. The spaghetti all arrabiatta is claimed to be, and probably is, the best on the island. During the club season the crème de la crème of international DJ's come here, to fill up on high-energy carbohydrates and test out the crowd, before heading off to start their sets. The conversation is punctuated with two-cheek air kisses; comic, sarcastic asides and in-jokes: "What IS she wearing?".

When guests return to their rooms in the first few rays of

the early sun, from „Pacha" or „El Divino", their temporary homes at Ocean Drive provide gentle visual refreshment. The spacious, glistening bathrooms are perfect after a hot and heavy night, kitted out with dark granite basins and chrome fittings. The sleek shower cells are constructed from clear glass.

All 38 guestrooms, designed by Semi Masso, have a luxuriously livable Spanish touch: soft sofas, warm wall tones and cheery chequered

patterns. An environment to relax in. The more generously sized suites have similar colour schemes, and offer extensive balconies from which guests can enjoy views across the harbour, as far as the sandstone castle of Ibiza Town. A reminder of a different side of the island, but every bit as laid back.

02

01 | The exterior of the hotel is hardly breathtaking, but then again it doesn't have to be. Its simple, functional architecture sets the scene for the cool, easy life inside the property.

02 | A perfect location in the heart of the city, direct on the marina and within walking distance of the best dance clubs.

03 | The Ocean Drive is a meeting point for DJ's and clubbers, before and after the night's events.

04 | 05 Bistro and bar.

06 | The lobby is full of design classics.

ca'n verdera | mallorca . spain

DESIGN: Pepe Frontera

At first sight comfortingly small, as far as the number of rooms are concerned, though big in terms of personality, individual care and all-round service – this would be a fitting description for the Ca'n Verdera guest house in the picturesque region of Fornalutx (pronounced Fornaloosch).

Individuality, creativity, pleasure and comfort – these are the four building blocks of the concept. For Anna Celma, service takes utmost priority. She personally deals with the needs and requests of all her guests, ensuring that they enjoy everything about their stay, not just the fascinating landscape and intricate architecture. The three-storey natural stone building, over 150 years old, is set in a quiet, privileged location in the north-west of the Tramuntana mountain range, embedded in an

originally Mediterranean landscape. It nestles quite unobtrusively into a secluded mountain slope in the middle of the village. The peaceful environment with its countless orange groves could have been made for secluded, relaxing holidays. Despite the absence of any hint of hectic activity, Fornalutx can easily be reached from Palma within 30 minutes.

The charm of the Ca'n Verdera guest house (the Green House) stems from the clash of Mallorcan architecture, modern design and avant-garde art. The latter is exhibited on the hotel premises, though the works are not experienced as they would be in a museum. Deliberate choices of location within the guest house allow viewers to develop a relationship between the work of art in question and the space they are in, enhancing the experience the property offers.

For their stay, guests can chose between six individually designed guest rooms in three different categories. The rooms are equipped with all the necessary comforts and the furnishings, depending on category, are elegant though not over the top. The garden, with its lush vegetation, the relatively large, wonderfully situated pool and the shady terrace are all perfect places for dreaming, relaxing and recuperating. Here, on hot days, guests can let the day drift by in all calmness, while sipping on a cool drink beneath palm trees, gazing across a colourful sea of flowers.

Should your stay not be purely for relaxation, and business interests also have to be taken into consideration, the meeting rooms, equipped with the latest in modern technology, can be relied upon. They were specially

designed for communicative, creative events, thus it can easily happen that the entire building is fully booked by a company for an extended weekend.

The guest house also has a great deal to offer in terms of culinary pleasure. The chef's Mediterranean creations are a delight for the eyes, nose and taste buds, all freshly prepared from traditional recipes, and complemented by an exquisite wine selection, drawn mainly from Spanish regions. Enjoy a vintage from the nearby Binissalem vineyards, either with a delicious morsel from the diverse menu, or simply to accompany a mellow Mallorcan evening.

01

01 | The property's extensive garden is almost impossible to imagine when one sees Ca'n Verdera from outside.

02 | From most rooms, guests can enjoy grandiose vistas across the surrounding landscape.

03 | Nouvelle Cuisine is not so much the order of the day as rustical, but excellent country cooking.

04 | The entrance to Ca'n Verdera is only indicated by a tiny sign – a tightly-kept secret.

05 | Paintings and objet d'arts enrich the interior.

06 | For a hotel with just six rooms, the pool is surprisingly large.

07 | The two-storey penthouse suite - an oasis of inspiration.

ca's xorc | mallorca . spain

DESIGN: Wolfgang Nikolaus Schmidt, Mariano Barcelo, Juan and Gregory Puigserver

It all began on a trip to buy antique furniture. The search brought Klaus Christian Ploenzke, ex-IBM systems developer and founder of IT company CSC Ploenzke AG, to the Mallorcan port of Soller; still a small, remote place at the start of the '90's. Getting to Soller was no easy task then, with the only route an arduously winding road, up and over the mountains that form a ridge along Mallorca's western side. For nearly twenty years tunnel-borers chewed away at the rock, finally completing a shortcut in 1995. Luck for Ploenzke and his family. Instead of discovering furniture, he discovered a town palace called Ca's Puers – a wonderful

building in a Snow White sleep, that was also up for sale.

That he was setting the foundations for a gastronomic family enterprise was something that Ploenzke could hardly have known, as he signed the land register to complete his purchase of the house. It didn't take long, however, before he found the perfect adviser for the development of his property, in the shape of Munich-based star chef, Eckart Witzigmann. Word of the new gourmet address, Ca's Puers, not only soon spread across the island, but also throughout Germany, from Munich to Hamburg. Ploenzke's own daughter, Britta,

was captured by the place. While living in Los Angeles and working at the central offices of CSC, she came to visit, liked what she saw and stayed. More or less, that is. In between, she completed an intensive study of the hospitality industry, learning about the details that make a hotel world-class, at the Kempinski in Marbella, Spain. Armed with this new knowledge, and the addition of a further property located on an adjacent hillside, Ca's Xorc, Britta's hotel career began with the management of two houses.

Turning left from the road to Port Soller, the route curves towards Deia, before narrowing

01 | Cuisine that's definitely worth the drive: the German star chef, Eckart Witzigmann, is the hotel's culinary advisor. Today, the restaurant offers creative Mallorquin food.

02 | Lemons straight from the hotel's trees.

03 | Main entrance.

04 | A touch of North Africa combined with Mediterranean flair. The hotel's director, Britta Ploenzke, sources many of the accessories in Morocco herself.

06

05

05 | 06 The covered inner courtyard is an inviting
mixture of kasbah and country house.

into tight u-bends that lead to Ca's Xorc. Surrounded by centuries-old olive trees, there it lies, an oil mill over 200 years old, that rises into the sight of approaching visitors like a vision. Once the car is parked, and the stones steps to the building climbed, one enters a refuge in the truest sense. Surrounded by warm, country design and a spectacular landscape, guests can gaze out as from an elevated throne, over the Serra de Tramuntana and its highest peak, the 1,443-metre-high Puig Major.

The balance that has been achieved between historical substance and luxurious renovation is exemplary, with Britta Ploenzke and her team always adding new details. When the hotel and restaurant business at Ca's Xorc started in Spring 2000, there were 10 guestrooms and suites, now there are 13. Progress, certainly, but the hotel remains small, intimate and exclusive, hugged in a complete complex large enough to disappear into. Whether on the terraces in the garden, under a lustrous

mixture of hanging plants or, when the weather brings a few much-appreciated rain clouds to Mallorca, indoors in the library or by the crackling fire.

All together, the atmosphere is soft, country romantic, without ever verging on the kitsch. Although lushly decorated, nothing is too much, not a single colour is wrong or distracting, none of the accessories leave one feeling that they could have been done without. From the locally hand-painted tiles on the white-

washed walls to the plump, stuffed Moroccan cushions, each new element is enjoyed. The guestrooms themselves are simply very, very comfortable, leaving the only problem being which one to choose. Thanks to time-honoured building techniques, each room has its own particular floor-plan and layout, and its own individual interior design.

07

08

09

07 | From the pool, one can look out across Port Soller to the Mediterranean Sea. To the right are the Tramuntana mountains.

08 | 09 Each of the 13 guestrooms has a unique floor plan, differing colours, materials and furnishing and its own particular view.

es convent | mallorca . spain

DESIGN: Antonio Esteva

01

This small but perfectly conceived guesthouse is located in the centre of Alcudia. Via the short motorway, the drive to the north-west end of the island from Palma de Mallorca takes a little less than an hour. Negotiating the pedestrianized centre of old Alcudia is another matter, and it is a good idea to either take local advice, or at least consult a good map, to avoid glares from strolling tourists or the attention of the Policia Local.

The old substance of Es Convent is in good condition, and shines with Mallorcan flair. Guests are welcomed in the hall, which is also a great start, with its spaciousness and classic design. One can choose from four large rooms, tightly limiting the number of guests, which in turn allows the owners to guarantee an intimate, private

atmosphere. This ambience makes a stay at Es Convent an act of relaxation, despite the town centre location. Alongside the four air-conditioned, comfortably furnished bedrooms, the property also has a restaurant, open not only to residents, but also the public, drawn in by its refined Mediterranean cuisine.

The house is typified by a reduction to simple, traditional pleasures – a theme that extends from the hotel's architecture to its menu. Overall, the emphasis is on slickness and functionality, with a splash of Spanish flavour. Pre-existing, exposed building materials have been left in their original state, reflecting the age of the original structure and spotlighting their earthy textures, whether in the cut-stone walls, the natural stone flooring, the dark wooden beams overhead

or the contrasting white-washed plaster. The warm colours and combinations encourage a contented sensation, augmented by plain, polished wood furniture, and heavy cotton and linen fabrics. The elements of the whole ease together, and sitting at breakfast over a coffee and sugar-dusted, succulent ensaimadas, the surroundings have the same effect as a very comfy, well-loved, old pair of shoes.

Es Convent is an authentic product of its location, unashamedly and deeply rooted in Mallorcan custom. Friendly, unassuming and open, the hotel offers an authentic experience to anyone with the right frame of mind to seek it out.

01 | 02 The slick architecture from Antonio Esteva has been somewh neutralised by the owners' decoration and plants…

03 | ...but his minimalist signature can still be seen.

04 | Rustic reduction: cut stone, white plastered walls and fresh linen.

05 | Stone is also the dominant material in the bathrooms.

06 | Eye-catching details in the remodelled property.

07 | With just four guestrooms, the term "hotel" is a little exaggerated, but the property has a lobby and a restaurant where the owners specialize in fresh fish dishes.

son bernadinet | mallorca . spain

DESIGN: Antonio Esteva

01 | Main entrance.

02 | The original structure is over 200 years old.

01

02

03

The region between Porreres and Campos on Mallorca can be best described as either slightly raised, or simply flat, making the location of this country hotel significantly different from the other fincas described in this book. What may be considered boring by mountain-climbers is just right for lovers of unspoilt countryside, far removed from the tourist trail. On a vaguely tarmaced road connecting these two villages in the south-east, a small sign for "Agrotourismo – Son Bernadinet" points to a somewhat better field track lying among an abundance of undergrowth. Guests arriving at dusk are welcomed in a most splendid and exclusive manner by well-positioned, subtle lights. During the day, however, after covering the first 100 metres of the lane, one begins to wonder whether this hidden driveway is leading in the right direction. Those who carry on driving for the next 100 metres without getting lost, or losing their nerve, are spoilt by wonderfully aesthetic views, whether in sunlight or moonlight. Although the building is originally well over 200 years old, a few effective clues can already be seen from the outside that this is the work of a very talented designer.

The publicity-shy, reserved Mallorcan architect, Antonia Esteva, has left the historic substance to a large extent untouched. Only minor interventions bear witness to contemporary architecture. Fresh white plaster around the window and door lintels, for example; the filigree frames and mullions, or the flower garden bordered by a symmetrical pergola with concrete pillars and steel beams. The owner's long-term friend – who re-built the family residence – has also carefully restored the façade. Stepping through the main entrance doors, between two high, narrow sash, is more reminiscent of a friendly, subdued entrance to a private country home.

03 | Although the owners, the Bonet family, have turned the farmhouse into a hotel, the have maintained the biological agriculture.

04 | A balanced mix of materials, contrasts of shadow and light. Antonio Esteva's style is displayed in this open living space.

05　　　　　　　　　　**06**

And with a total of four rooms in the main building and a further seven converted rooms in former stables, this would not be too far removed from the truth.

Despite it being hugely popular and excellently suited to families with small children, the place is never really bustling with activity. It maintains a sense of calm and a high degree of privacy. "Properly informal" is probably a good description. This is first and foremost due to its charming hosts: mother, Francisca Bonet, and daughter, Alicia Fernández, together with their friendly team. A team who make staying here pleasurable and uncomplicated,

but also educational. Not only can a great deal be learned about the history of Mallorca and the development of the rural population, but also about the refined local cuisine. Whether at open-air barbecues or in the cosy dining room, delicious evening meals are served prepared with fresh, home-grown, organic ingredients.

Both mother and daughter possess the graceful beauty of noble landed gentry, though they modestly deny this. They do, however, like to reminisce about their very long Mallorcan family tradition, Francisca maybe telling an anecdote or two over a glass of wine, spiced with philosophical observations on

07

07

05 | 06 The partially roofed terrace functions as an outdoor lounge. Right next to this is a water pool – not for swimming – and beyond are the fields.

07 | Corridor through the hotel's public areas.

08 | Antonio Esteva mixes a blend of old stone, traditional white plaster and antiques, set off against modern furnishings.

08

09

10   11   12   13

09 | Stairs to the roof balcony, from where one   10 | From outside, classic finca…   11 | …but from inside, sophisticated design…   12 | 13 …and typical Mallorquin style
can enjoy the breathtaking view.

14

14 |15 Cieling, walls and floors provide the perfect frame for an aethstetic play between

colours, shadow and accessories.

15

son pons | mallorca . spain

DESIGN : Manfred Tumfart

01

To be permanently on holiday in one of the most beautiful corners of the world – who wouldn't dream of it? A dream of an orderly little finca that one could share as a guesthouse with interesting visitors, finally being able to realise, as a host, all those ideas never acted upon before. Ingrid Wolter not only longed for this idyll, but actually threw in her job as a teacher to pursue it. With a few

bags, and her grown-up daughter Astrid, she moved to the family's holiday location in the north-west of the island. Helped by her brother-in-law, Manfred Tumfart, professor of interior design at Mainz Technical College, she managed to create a sparkling gem from the historical estate, its history spanning back to the 13th Century, perfect for those seeking relaxation. With only

five rooms, or rather suites, Son Pons is an insider tip best kept to oneself…or shared with just a few close friends.

The house's familiar atmosphere and minimalist, refined design, its architectonic and gastronomic concept primarily attracts guests looking for aesthetics, seclusion and uncomplicated service. Exactly the kind of people that the

hosts want around them. Most of us know that dreams and reality are worlds apart, and the Wolter women obviously didn't book an eternal holiday either. Quite the opposite, with this kind of family business working around the clock is an indispensable sacrifice, especially when living under the same roof as the paying guests. Despite all the hard work, the trained teacher is still fully

02

03

04

05

01 | Walkway to the courtyard -
   natural materials in harmony.

02 | The family-run house with just
   five guestrooms is easily
   accesible from the main
   Palma–Alcudia road.

03 | The building's roots go back to
   the 13th Century.

04 | There is no restaurant, but Ingrid
   Wolters often cooks up a relaxed
   dinner for guests.

06

05 | Among lush vegetation hides the
   hotel's narrow lap pool.

06 | Courtyard with original well.

motivated in her new role after the first season: "We've learnt a lot and are having a lot of fun." For Ingrid Wolter good service does not mean having three different types of cognac available in an ugly minibar, but rather a cosy breakfast with fresh eggs from the neighbouring farmer. Or even creating a festive menu should the occasion require it. She carefully enhances her brother-in-law's simple architecture with tasteful decorations. Even if she does pass on all the credit for the design to her sister's husband, her instinctive and confident treatment of the aesthetic space he has created

is more than evident at all times.

Manfred Tumfart has reflected the history of the house. A great deal of its original charm has been left intact. Thus the estate radiates an historic charm which somehow or other is very appealing. Details that were more or less hidden previously, even if only the structure of the stonework, have been skilfully brought to the fore, using sunken spotlights in the flooring, for example. Previously shady corners have been given a new touch using pale colours, glass surfaces or openings to let in light. The corridor through the

gradually developed complex, with trails leading off in all directions – here an annex, there an extension – offers a tour through an aesthetic labyrinth. In between are an idyllic, village square-like courtyard, a wild garden which is either cared for or kept under control, no-one seems quite sure, and finally, the long narrow swimming pool. It is beautiful out in the open. Nevertheless, Son Pons is a finca where simply lounging in the rooms is a pleasure, in their spacious and very homely ambience.

Son Pons is situated in close proximity to the northern

bathing resorts of Port d'Alcudia and Port de Pollença at the edge of the village, Campanet-Ullaro. Easily reachable in half an hour's drive on the main road from Palma to Alcudia, the magical estate is conveniently located. Watch local farmers tend their potatoes, onions and artichokes in the nearby fields of Sa Pobla, visit the spectacular caves at Campanet, or venture out to Muro for a traditional lunch. When you manage to leave Son Pons, there's plenty to fill the day before you can finally return to your new-found home.

07 | 11 Each of the five rooms has been individually designed by the professor for interior design at the Mainz Technical College, Manfred Tumfart.

san roque | tenerife . spain

DESIGN: José Luis Adelantado

01

Set in the picturesque town of Garachico, in the north of Tenerife, Hotel San Roque is the end result of a "wonderful friendship" which began between the French hotel veteran of 30 years, Dominque Carayon, and a splendid 17th-century manor house in the centre of this 6,000 strong town. Delicately renovated for four years under the watchful eye and management of Dominique's friend, the Valencian interior architect Luis Adelantado, many of the original materials in the house

were salvaged and reused in the remodelling. The wooden flooring was an example of this, and proved to be a source of both joy and frustration. The rich brown Canary pine, from which it is constructed, is particularly strong thanks to a saltwater treatment that the boards had undergone centuries before. In this old method of preservation, which is no longer carried out due to the time and cost, the planks were stored in seawater for some years, which allowed the salt to impregnate the wood,

making them extremely durable. Although the result is a wonderful building material, its toughness was a problem for the local carpenters who worked on the restoration, as machine after machine jammed or simply broke when confronted with the cured pine. It seemed that their modern electric saws were no match for their ancestors' old-fashioned tools and muscle-power.

Arranged around the inner courtyard, the San Roque's 20 bright, and spacious room are

each designed with a different colour scheme, furnished with modern classics by Le Corbusier, Charles Rennie Mackintosh, Marcel Breuer, Eileen Gray or Mies van der Rohe. The interior architecture shows a versatile interplay between colour and form, tradition and innovation, liberally laced with artworks from Spanish artists. All bathrooms come equipped with jacuzzi tubs, and anyone who can spare the funds should experience the Turret Suite - a reason alone for flying to the island.

02   03

04

01 | The San Roque's logo, with palm and olive tree.

02 | The hotel is formed around the courtyard and swimming pool.

03| An example of the modern furnishings.

04 | Guests lounge in the terrace-like corridors…

05 | …and sleep in the just as intensively coloured rooms and suites. All 20 have a jacuzzi tub in the bathroom.

05

07

06 | 07 The lobby / lounge's contemporary seating
complements the centuries-old building.

08 | The hotel's furnishings are largely drawn from
classic designs by, among others, Marcel Breuer,
Le Corbusier and Eileen Gray.

08

riders palace | laax . switzerland

DESIGN: René Meierhofer

01

01 | Hi-tech among the mountains, Riders Palace is the newest destination for the snowboarding Generation @.

02 | Wood, steel and glass are the main building materials.

Hype has entered the quiet world of the mountains, and who else could be to blame but the snowboarders. These guys, like an Alpine tribe of surfers, are simply different to those mere mortals who need two skis to bring them down the piste. Wherever they meet, there's something going on, and it's clear that a traditional "Heidi-style" chalet is not going to cut the mustard, whether as a place to sleep or a place to party.

The Riders Palace, in the Swiss resort of Laax, was conceived as the ultimate answer to the requirements of the snowboarder community. "Hyperactive, super connected and very international" is how the hotel describes its own clients. As the first high-tech hotel in the Alps, it offers the multimedia Generation@ every form of digital entertainment. Video beamer, DVD cinema and high-speed internet stations are all standard. Then come, according to choice of room, a multimedia package, Dolby Digital surround system, PlayStation2 and a plasma screen TV. But that's up to each guest, and here, right next to the ski-lift station in Laax, Riders Palace has a bed to suit each budget and taste. For those who snowboard all day and club all night, there's the youth hostel type "Back to Basics" option, in shared rooms with four to seven beds. If sleeping late, and breakfast in bed is more on the agenda, the hotel offers luxury apartments and suites for two. Seventy rooms, with a total of 312 beds, are available altogether.

In design, even the Back to Basics accomodation is young and stylish. Bathroom fittings

02

03 | Openness and simplicity are part of the interior concept. Bathroom and toilet are separated from bedroom by a thin, transparent wall.

06 | The building, with its almost ephemeral appearance, is just a few steps away from the ski lifts.

04 | 05 A total of 312 beds are available in 70 rooms.

03

and wash basins gleam in cool chrome, and the ceilings lend an urban edge, with their visible concrete. An exceptional windowed front gives a view to the very reasons that one comes to Riders Palace: the mountains, the snow and the half-pipe. In the luxury suites and apartments, the interior architecture and furnishing is naturally a little more plush. Large, white, inviting beds; generous, open-plan bathrooms; "Steely Weaver" lamps create a magical light and comfy seating cubes and sofas beg to be lounged on for hours. A natural

place to dream about the day gone by…if you manage to find the time!

Although that might not be as easy as you'd think. The bar at Riders Palace is open 24 hours a day, and is also the lobby and reception, functioning as a central meeting place. On the weekend, the Palace Club becomes home to the legendary, London-based Ministry of Sound, setting up the atmosphere for an open-ended party where sleep is the last resort. And reservations? Via the internet…of course.

04

05

06

al porto | lachen . switzerland

DESIGN: Piero Lissoni

Had Andy Rihs, manager, wine grower and cattle breeder, not needed new office space, who knows whether Al Porto would exist today. In his search for the right location, he discovered a run-down building from the '70s, in Lachen, on the banks of Lake Zurich. Although already being used as a hotel at the time, Rihs saw potential for some vast improvements.

With Piero Lissoni as designer, Rihs found a dream partner for his new concept. Taking advantage of the fantastic location near the water's edge, an Italian inspired ambience was moulded, dedicated to pleasure and la Dolce Vita – a simple formula that has become a resounding success. Today, Al Porto, with its twelve rooms and five junior suites is a small, beautiful place. Andy

Rihs even furnished two rooms in the same building as his office, breaking the rule, and mixing business with pleasure.

The hotel's entrance appears unpretentious and inconspicuous, a little secretive, not revealing the interior. It is symbolic for the unobtrusive style of the hotel, in terms of its design, and also in terms of service. In the lobby, enormous

bamboo stems greet the arriving guests. Placed right by the glass front, they form a soft border between inside and outside, gently shielding from external gazes. Wide sofas and deep armchairs in black and white are casually placed around the room, and white '60s-style side tables, small stools and paper lamps create smart accents and a relaxed feel. The shiny floors reflect the

02

03

01 | On the banks of Lake Zurich, the construction dates from the 1970's.

02 | 03 Innovative and aethstetic – the bamboo stems provide definition to the lobby space, creating transparency but also an effect of protection.

04 | The kitchen is surrounded by glass, allowing diners to see straight into the chef's pans.

05 | View across Lake Zurich from one of the five junior suites.

04

furniture, the bamboo and the guests, mirroring the interior scene, much as the lake mirrors the landscape outside.

The blurring of spacial borders is a recurring theme in Al Porto. Glass was clearly a favourite material for the planners, allowing them to produce a playful tension between transparency and unity. The ground floor illustrates this idea, and is not only open to the hotel's guests, but also to the public. Its restaurant, café and bar offer a range of culinary experiences, the Italian flavour remaining as a common denominator throughout. Separate areas are connected and related through carefully arranged sightlines. Glass walls surround the restaurant's show kitchen, turning the area into a theatrical stage, with guests eagerly spectating as their meals are conjured up before them. Cobbled terraces, with modern wood furniture and covered with tangled arbours, stretch toward the lake's shore. The ingenious frontage can be lowered into the ground to form a sheltered open-air space, letting in the mild climate during the summer months.

Just like the restaurant, café and bar, the rooms are located on the first floor and they too are an expression of cheerful ease. The colour scale is neutral: light carpets, clean white bed linen, crème-coloured curtains and padded furniture in greys and beiges, all contrasting against a black painted wall. Red sideboards create tone accents here and there. Sharp lines and simple shapes characterize the elegant style. In a world that bombards us with its huge variety of sensory impressions, such simplicity can direct one to the substantial. The extensive glazing does this, directing guests' views towards the waters of Lake Zurich.

05

06 | Defined, separated colours and brightness are common to all 17 rooms.

07 | Restaurant with Italian cuisine.

08 | Bar.

04

In addition, some rooms have their own timber-floored terraces, a hint at where to sit to watch the sunset.

With its reduction to the elementary, Al Porto has succeeded in creating a bright and vivacious ambience. Enjoyment is the keyword, without reservation, but without sumptuous excess. Content is what matters for Al Porto, and that in a wonderfully wrapped parcel.

07
08

saratz | pontresina . switzerland

DESIGN: Hans-Jörg Ruch

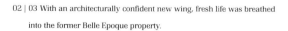

01 | Regardless of generation or social grouping, the Saratz is a vibrant mixing-pot for its guests.

02 | 03 With an architecturally confident new wing, fresh life was breathed into the former Belle Epoque property.

The hotel as a stage, nature as a grandiose backdrop, guests and staff as actors… perhaps that's why the General Manager is called "Direktor" in German? And which play is to be performed tonight? That changes each evening, and depends on the right blend of people. Achieving the right mixture is Adrian Stalder's talent. As "Direktor" of the Saratz, he brings the best

jazz musicians for concerts, invites the most renowned painters and sculptors to exhibit their work and allows the Swiss comic artist, Andrea Caprez, to create ironic Saratz scenes. There is no doubt, Adrian Stalder is the prince that has kissed awake this once sleeping Belle Epoque hotel. Its success story began more than five years ago, when the time-faded

grand hotel received its new, cubist, sand-coloured wing.

Swiss architect, Hans-Joerg Ruch, developed a large, clearly composed structure, without any compromising decorative elements. As the designer himself says, however, the wing is by no means a "furnished cow shed", and creates a link

to the main, original 1920's building. A low joining section, with glass façade, makes the bridge between new and old, giving a breathtaking, framed view of the Roseg glacier. Zurich-based architect, Pia Schmid, was responsible for the expansive hall with its powerful open fireplaces, and the bar's wonderfully calm, contemporary design. She sprinkled the rooms with pieces from Swiss artists, while choosing light, flexible furniture such as Arne Jacobson's classic "Seven" chairs. Guests should be able to arrange the furniture to their own needs.

The existing buildings were freed from centimetres of old paint and ugly floor coverings, and were gently, carefully restored. To add a special bite, artists Ivan and Basil Lugenbühl produced a slightly bizarre bar counter from the left over scrap iron, stairway railings, old metal wall ladders, pots and pans. In the new Saratz, a rare atmosphere has taken over, where every generation feels welcome and comfortable, from trendy media insiders to seasoned antique lawyers. Relaxation is available to each and every guest in the 3.5 hectare park that surrounds the hotel, with its dramatic gorge. The modern indoor pool, from which swimmers can gaze out across the parklands, together with a sauna and sun terrace, is enjoyed by everyone, whichever character they may be playing on the day.

04

05 | 06

04 | Lobby with open fireplace.

05 | 06 Indoor pool with views across the hotel's 3.5 hectares of parkland.

07 | Not just form and material, but also light can have a major
effect on a building's architectural character.

08 | All of the 63 rooms share a fantastic panorama of the
Alpine landscape.

08

yunak evleri | ürgüp . turkey

DESIGN: Cavit Kartal

01

Generally, one imagines life as a caveman to be fairly uncomfortable, yet it continues to have a certain attraction, especially to some city people. In Australia, examples of habitable caves can still be found today, and in the Turkish region of Cappadocia, this form of shelter enjoys a long tradition. As early as the 5th Century, people dug their housing out of the area's soft tuff, formed as a result of volcanic activity.

At the beginning of the '90's, in the provincial town of Ürgüp, entrepreneur Yusuf Gorurgoz bought a number of cave dwellings from their inhabitants, who were more than happy to be able to move into "normal" houses. It took Gorurgoz, together with a team of architects and restaurateurs, four years to transform the houses into a hotel complex. Today it is without doubt one of the most extraordinary guesthouses in Europe.

On the southern side of a large cliff high above the town are caverns and niches, stairs and windows dug deep in the rock. Terraces are stacked up precariously on various levels; at first glance an almost surreal sight for urban eyes so used to angled surroundings. But a deep inner order, the harmony of a developed structure, soon becomes apparent to guests and contributes largely to a special atmosphere.

The reception and dining rooms are situated outside of the caves in a Greek-style manor house dating back to the 19th Century. From here, guests reach their accommodation via small off-set courtyards and various steps. With its 15 rooms and two suites, the Yunak Evleri is a relatively small hotel but the extensiveness of the complex guarantees the utmost peace and an optimally large private sphere. According to the architect's taste, some of the rooms are vaulted, some rectangular, and all are dominated by a subdued, modern Mediterranean style. The dark wooden floors and furniture have not been confected in a fake rustic style, but are plainly elegant and practical. Cupboards built into the wall, and the light-coloured tuff and pure white linen fit the conventional ideal of a southern way of life, mirroring the character and cycles of the surrounding countryside. Lecterns and niches are typical elements of these habitable caves and make each room an original. The terrace offers a breathtaking view of the town – one could sit here for hours, with a glass of wine or sweet Turkish tea, enjoying the heavenly peace and quiet.

A curious atmosphere dominates this place. On the one hand it has a natural, unspoilt feel, and on the other hand boasts all the thoroughly modern comforts of a first-class hotel. In some corners, one seems far removed from any kind of civilisation. Candles burn in small hollows and the coarsely cut walls and rough stone appear to originate from another epoch. Folkloristic elements such as embroidery and carvings round off this picture. When one encounters the bathroom with its marble and very modern splendour, it's not unusual to feel somewhat confused by this odd, somehow harmonious contrast.

At Yunak Evleri one tends not to enquire about technical comforts, although they are naturally available. Telephone, internet and fax service are all classed as average, although air-conditioning is certainly not necessary in these naturally cool caves.

The hotel's name means "Well Houses" and is also the name of this whole quarter of town. Prior to the conversion, people actually lived here without running water, heating or modern comforts. The daily life of women was played out at the market place and at the well. In contrast to this, life as a modern-day cave dweller can be positively luxurious. The previous residents would certainly no longer recognise their homes.

02

03

01 | Caverns and niches, steps and windows all carved from
deep within the stone.

02 | A typical interior.

03 | The hotel lies high above the town of Ürgüp.

04 | Before their renovation, these cave houses were the homes
of local inhabitants.

05 | Each of the 15 rooms is unique. The deisgn is dominated by
a reserved, modern Mediterranean style.

04

05

the tresanton | cornwall . united kingdom

DESIGN: Olga Polizzi

01 | Wild greenery and steep cliffs make a wonderful partnership with the mild, Gulf Stream climate.

02 | Wellington boots and other accessories can be bought under the hotel's own "Onda" label.

Not far from Land's End, where thick polo neck sweaters, rubber boots and oil skins belong to basic clothing equipment, for many overseas guests, the Tresanton may seem a surprising choice for relaxation. But, as the locals and English visitors have known for generations, there is no finer location to absorb undiluted, all-powerful nature at her purest.

The south-western county of Cornwall has a distinct character, and a rich history of stories and legends. The Cornish toast "Fish, tin and copper", indicates what were once the crucial elements in the everyday life of the local people. Although this may have changed over the years, the raw, almost primeval landscape, warmed by the Gulf Stream, is still littered with villages that are reminders of Cornwall's past. St. Mawes is just such a place.

This quiet fishing village, with its fortress of the same name high above the rocky bay, is the area's main attraction. Each morning, day tourists arrive to marvel the impressive castle established in 1543 by Henry VIII for the defence of the coast. Almost as much a part of the village as the fort is the family of Lord Shawcross, Britain's chief prosecutor at the Nurnberg Trials. His son, William Shawcross, political journalist and international relations expert, was no stranger to the beauty of St. Mawes when he met Olga Polizzi, daughter of Lord Forte, founder of the eponymous hotel group. An experienced and respected hotel interior designer herself, Polizzi was central in the positioning of her brother Rocco Forte's own hotel collection, built after the old Forte group left the family's hands in the mid 1990's. Despite Rocco's fine portfolio of

luxury houses located in Britain, Russia, Belgium, Italy and Germany, it was in Cornwall, in St. Mawes, that Olga discovered her personal idyll.

Built in 1940 as a yacht club, next door to the Shawcross holiday home, the Tresanton today presents itself as a collection of individual buildings, situated at differing heights. During the '50's it was considered one of the most well-known and most popular hotels in Cornwall, but lost much of its radiant aura over the course of the following decades. It started to regain its lost pride, becoming a well-kept secret for London society, once Polizzi and Shawcross acquired it in 1997 and invested in the cluster of houses. After extensive renovation and reorganization, Olga inspired the estate to new life, with its country house style dominated by bright colours.

The designers were guided in their concept for the interior by the natural brilliance of the location, and developed a whole design line exclusively for the Tresanton, ranging from wall coverings to floors and ceilings, to the furniture and lighting, through to the table decorations. The style mainly draws on maritime models - the prevailing material is wood, usually painted in white and combined with different shades of blue. The range has become so popular with hotel guests that Polizzi's children, Alex and Charlie, have since opened the "Onda" shop in the village, selling accessories, clothing and furniture either directly from or inspired by the Tresanton. If you're not lucky enough to be able to experience the shop or the hotel in the near future, as taste of what you're missing can be found at: ondaonline.co.uk

03 | In the former St. Mawes yacht club there are now 28 guestrooms.

04 | With their individual styling, the bedrooms have the charm of a private house.

05 | Olga Polizzi's designs are marked by restrained pastel tones and soft forms.

06 | For floors and walls, wood in different colours is the main material.

seaham hall | seaham . united kingdom

DESIGN: Kappers Architects

01

Located on England's east coast in the county of Yorkshire, Seaham Hall can be reached in a two-hour drive from Edinburgh, or in three hours by express train from London. The wild countryside of the surrounding area is the perfect backdrop for discovering the region, with nearby Hadrian's Wall or the county's historical capital, York. The house itself was built in 1792, and in 1815 witnessed the wedding of Lord George Gordon Byron to Annabella Milbanke, daughter of Sir Ralph Milbanke. Lord Byron is one of England's most renowned Romantic poets, whose work achieved popular acclaim even during his own lifetime.

The estate is sandwiched between two very different natural situations. On the one side is the rugged North Sea coast, on the other an undulating, hilly landscape full of forests and cliffs. In the midst of this, the opening of oriental baths at Seaham Hall is an unusual attraction for a property so steeped in local tradition. Carved into the rock on which the hotel sits, The Spa, with its teak-clad interior, offers an Asian ambience with spectacular waterworks. An underground path directly connects the grotto housing the spa complex to the hotel, and a watercourse accompanies guests on their way through the darkness, setting the mood for the refreshing and decadent pleasures to come. A 20-metre-long swimming pool, hot springs and a waterfall are merely a few of the highlights of the magical cavern, which also offers Thai massage, various cosmetic treatments and even an Asian cookery course.

02

01 | Two hours by car from Edinburgh, the hotel lies in the county of Yorkshire.

02 | Many details point to the East - West design mix.

03 | The lobby's cieling, designed by stained-glass artist, Bridget Jones.

03

04 | 05 Western elegance is contrasted by Asian flair.　　06 | Five differing types of room can be chosen from, from deluxe to penthouse suite.　　07 | Shower with a view.

Nineteen individually designed rooms, fully air-conditioned and luxuriously furnished, await the hotel guest. As standard expect a Bang & Olufsen TV with 100 channels, in addition to internet access, a direct dial telephone and fax machine. Furthermore, guests are able to hold video conferences or multimedia presentations in four private conference rooms, which can accomodate 120 visitors altogether. This arrangement especially recommends Seaham Hall to companies wishing to hold their congresses and seminars in a relaxed environment.

Guests can choose between more or less extravagant rooms according to their taste and budget. The categories range from single suite to deluxe and superior, to penthouse. All the rooms are equipped with a large bathroom with double washbasin and a bathtub big enough for two. Optically, the rooms are strong, but tasteful and slightly reminiscent of a neo-Biedermeier style. With their matching colours and sensitively coordinated material, however, they are soothing on the eye and appear more modern than antiquated.

The public areas around the reception, lobby, staircases and restaurant as well as the parking lot also serve as an art gallery for paintings and sculptures, the main focus being on regional and Norwegian artists. Especially worth seeing is the ceiling of the atrium-type lobby designed by the stained-glass artist, Bridget Jones.

08 | Conferences and meetings count are part of Seaham Hall's daily busine.

09 | All rooms have CD player.

10 | Light and shadow are used as deliberate design elements.

11 | The majority of furnishings were specially commissioned.

12 | Decoration is limited to carefully chosen pieces.

13 | Romanticism plays an important role at the hotel – every room has a two-person bathtub.

12

13

babington house | somerset . united kingdom

DESIGN: Simon Morray-Jones

01   02

01 | 02 Babington House lies 120 miles south-west of London in the county of Somerset. It already existed in the 14th Century, as the country seat of the Cheddar family.

03 | Today, the building houses 28 guestrooms for city-dwellers longing for a few days of rural peace.

04 | The free-standing bathtubs found in all roms.

05 | Log Room with rustic, Italian inspired cuisine.

06 | The design is modern but not modernistic. Here, another example of the bathrooms.

03   04

Generally, one would imagine staying in an historic English county to be very romantic. Far removed from the hassle of the city, with long walks, croquet and horse riding, and cosy evenings in front of an open fire. Many country guest houses in the British hinterland play on this image, though rarely hold up to their promises. Stuffy service and a rigorous denial of all things modern-day seem, for many, to pass as excentricity.

This miserable situation may have been one reason why Soho House Country, sister to the company which runs the renowned Soho House private members club in central London, decided to create a similar, provincial version of their ideal, out of a magnificent property roughly 120 miles south-west of London. The site of Babington House in the county of Somerset was established in the 14th Century as the country seat of the Cheddar family. In the course of time, the property changed hands and was repeatedly converted, until it was sold in the mid-'90's to Soho House Country – a decision which has proven to be a blessing for all concerned. Not only can its own club members holiday here, befitting their club status, but us normal citizens can also find refuge.

With its classical cream-coloured façade, its small chapel and the lush surrounding landscape, the property does indeed fulfil romantic notions of the country idyll. Inside, a completely new interpretation of the "country club" theme is found. Not only has the stuffy atmosphere been replaced in favour of a more open, lively design, but the staff have no hint of formality about them either. Sofas with zebra patterns add to an amusing, kitsch, retro style which greets the guests in the entrance hall. The Manager himself makes a very laid-back impression, and evidently feels very much at ease.

Twenty-seven rooms are distributed over various wings of the house, some of them specially designed with families with children in mind. The rooms in the attic are inspired by a low-key Italian style. The oak floors and the simple wooden furniture appear classic and attractively elementary in the wide, open layout. In contrast, the rooms on the first floor play with popular set pieces, such as a free-standing Victorian bathtub. Every room is equipped with a wide-screen

television with DVD player and top-of-the-range stereo system. This bonus, on top of the usual extras, can be explained by the fact that most members of the Soho House club are media and film professionals. In addition to media work areas, the hotel's own 45-seater cinema draws guests in every evening with showings of the latest films as well as old classics.

In view of these extras, it is almost superfluous to mention the first-class service – what else would one expect? Apart from the pool and tennis courts, the property includes a former cowshed where guests can participate in an extensive wellness programme. A whole range of treatments is offered together with products made on the estate. After indulging oneself here for an afternoon, guests could be enticed by an evening meal in the Log Room or, on mild evenings, on the terrace, to see the day out in al-fresco style. The food at Babington House is honest, rustic, true country fare with plenty of tasty grill and oven-baked specialities, and international influences also putting in a few appearances. The menu changes weekly and is mainly determined by the region's sellers who contribute differing ingredients according to the season.

So how does one get to enjoy all these comforts? True, Babington House is, in the first instance, a private club with local residents, within 30 miles, also being eligible to apply for membership. To avoid the influx of people into the region rising dramatically however, the gates of the estate are open to all those looking for something different and a change from the standard romantic country house feel.

Country	City	Address	Information	Architecture & Design	Page

Austria	St. Anton	Aparthotel Anton 6580 St. Anton am Arlberg Austria http://www.anton-aparthotel.com	opened 2000 16 rooms including 2 apartments Anton Bar, Anton Square and Anton Café large roof garden, glazed roof-top sauna and steam bath located right at the Galzig mountain lift's valley station, serving the Valluga ski area	Wolfgang Pöschl + Büro	8
France	Bordeaux	Saint James 3, place Camille Hostein 33270 Bouliac France http://www.jm-amat.com	opened 1989 15 rooms, 3 apartments restaurant, café and bistro conference facilities, swimming pool located in the east of Bordeaux	Jean Nouvel	10
France	Gascogny	Castelnau Des Fiuemarcon 32700 Lagarde France	opened 2002 a 13th-century village 34 suites distributed among 16 cottages restaurant meeting room situated between Toulouse and Bordeaux	Frédéric Coustols	12
France	Laguiole	Hotel Michel Bras Route de l'Aubrac 12210 Laguiole France http://www.michel-bras.com	opened 1993 15 rooms gourmet restaurant and lounge golf course 170 km to Clermont-Ferrand and 60 km to the airport at Rodez	Eric Raffy	16
France	St. Tropez	Maison Blanche Place des Lices 83990 St - Tropez France http://www.hotellamaisonblanche.com	opened 1985 5 rooms and 4 junior suites champagne bar located in the centre of St. Tropez	Fabienne Villacréces	20
Germany	Lütgenhof	Schloss Lütgenhof Ulmenweg 10 23942 Dassow Germany http://www.schloss-luetgenhof.de	opened 1999 23 guest rooms gourmet restaurant, "Jägermeister" bar conference room for up to 42 people banquets for up to 100 people located close to the lake at Dassow, between Lübeck and Wismar	Schwarzenberg Deutsche Werkstätten in Dresden-Hellerau	22
Germany	Helgoland	Atoll Lung Wai 27 27498 Helgoland Germany http://www.atoll.de	opened 1999 51 guestrooms including 5 suites restaurant, bistro, cafe, Atoll Sansibar wellness area with massage and reiki, indoor pool and fitness room 2 conference rooms located in the south of Helgoland	Alison Brooks Architects	24
Germany	Hornbach	Kloster Hornbach im Klosterbezirk 66500 Hornbach Germany http://www.kloster-hornbach.de	opened 2000 34 rooms including 3 suites and 2 coach rooms restaurant "ProVence", monastery tavern and beer garden swimming area with sauna, steam bath and plunge pool 4 event rooms for up to 100 people situated between Saarbrücken and Pirmasens, close to the French border	Klaus Meckler Ralph Flum	28

Country	City	Address	Information	Architecture & Design	Page
Germany	Nakenstorf	Seehotel Nakenstorf Seestr. 1 23992 Nakenstorf Germany http://www.seehotel-neuklostersee.de	opened 1992 13 rooms, 1 apartment and 3 holiday homes restaurant with large terrace boathouse for events with up to 20 people, seminar- and conference rooms; sauna and massage located close to Neuklostersee, 2.5 hours to Berlin and 2 hours to Hamburg	Nalbach + Nalbach Gernot and Johanne Nalbach	30
Germany	Schneverdingen	Camp Reinsehlen 29640 Reinsehlen / Schneverdingen Germany http://www.campreinsehlen.de	opened 1999 38 rooms, 28 with private terrace hotel lobby with bar, bistro and chimney ecologically oriented restaurant conference rooms for 15 to 250 people located in the "Lüneburger Heide", between Hamburg and Bremen	Bernd R. Nalleweg Kristian Lemburg	32
Italy	Cattolica	Carducci 76 Viale Carducci, 76 47841 Cattolica Italy http://www.carducci76.it	opened 2000 28 rooms and 10 suites restaurant "Vicolo Santa Lucia" heated pool and yoga gardens, fitness room and spa 15 min to Riccione, between Bologna and Cattolica	Luca Sgroi	34
Italy	Florence	Villa Fontelunga Via Cunicchio No. 5 Foiano della Chiana 52045 Arezzo Italy	opened 2000 9 rooms swimming pool, tennis court located in Tuscany, 1 hour to Florence by car	Philipp Robinson	36
Portugal	Alcácer do Sal	Pousada Dom Afonso II 7580 Alcácer do Sal Portugal http://www.pousadas.pt	opened 1998 33 guestrooms and 2 suites restaurant and bar serving traditional Portuguese fare swimming pool, lots of outdoor facilities nearby conference room for up to 140 people located to the north of Lisbon, 1 hour by car	Diogo Pimentel	38
Portugal	Amares	Pousada Santa Maria do Bouro 4720-688 Amares Portugal http://www.pousadas.pt	built 1162, re-opened 1997 30 guestrooms and 2 suites restaurant, bar serving regional dishes conference facilities for up to 100 people situated between the Peneda Gerês National Park and the city of Braga	Eduardo Souto de Moura	40
Portugal	Arraiolos	Pousada de Nossa Senhora da Assunção Apartado 61 7040-909 Arraiolos Portugal http://www.pousadas.pt	built 1527, re-opened 1996 32 guestrooms including suites restaurant and bar serving authentic local cuisine swimming pool, many outdoor facilities nearby conference facilities for up to 120 people located to the west of Lisbon, 130 km by car	José Paulo dos Santos	44
Portugal	Cascais	Farol Design Hotel Av. Rei Humberto II de Italia, 7 2750-461 Cascais Portugal http://www.cascais.org	opened 2002 35 guestrooms including suites restaurant, several bars, club for 600 people, sun-bed terrace outdoor pool, hammam spa, steam bath and roof-top jacuzzi business centre with 2 conference rooms located in the centre of Cascais, 23 km from Lisbon International Airport	CM Dias Arquitectos LDA	48

Country	City	Address	Information	Architecture & Design	Page
Portugal	Crato	Pousada Flor da Rosa 7430-999 Crato Portugal http://www.pousadas.pt	built 1356, reopened 1995 24 rooms including suites restaurant and bar serving authentic local cuisine pool, billiard table and many outdoor facilities 130 km west of Lisbon	Carrilho da Graça	52
Portugal	Madeira	Choupana Hills Resort & Spa Travessa do Largo da Choupana 9050-286 Funchal Portugal http://www.choupanahills.com	opened 2002 60 deluxe rooms and 4 suites Xôpana Restaurant, Basalt Bar, pool bar and lounge health and beauty spa, 2 swimming pools, outdoor jacuzzi seminar room up to 40 people located in the verdant hillsides of Funchal, near the bay	Didier Lefort	56
Portugal	Madeira	Crowne Plaza Resort Estrada Monumental, 175-177 9000-100 Funchal Portugal http://www.madeira.crowneplaza.com	opened 2000 276 guestrooms, 24 suites several restaurants, bars and cafe spa, golf course, 9 meeting rooms up to 200 people southern coast of Madeira, 20 minute walk to Funchal	Ricardo Nogueira Duarte Caldeira Silva Massa Cinzenta, Lda	60
Portugal	Madeira	Estalagem da Ponta do Sol Quinta da Rochinha 9360-121 Funchal Portugal http://www.pontadosol.com	opened 2001 54 guestrooms with balcony and seaview restaurant, bar, poolside snackbar and cafe 2 pools, steam bath, jacuzzi and gym situated on the south coast of Madeira, 20 minute drive to Funchal	Tiago Oliveira	64
Portugal	Madeira	Quinta da Casa Branca Rua da Casa Branca, No. 7 9000-088 Funchal Portugal http://www.quintacasabranca.pt	opened 1999 / 2002 29 rooms, 12 deluxe rooms and 2 king suites 2 restaurants, 2 bars swimming pool, big tropical garden, spa and jacuzzi located in the town centre of Funchal	João Favila Menezes Teresa Goes Ferreira	70
Spain	Ibiza	Ocean Drive Hotel Playa de Talamanca Apt. 223 07800 Ibiza Spain http://www.oceandrive.de	opened 1998 38 guestrooms including 2 suites most rooms have ocean view and balcony Ocean Drive restaurant and bar directly on the Botafoch Marina, 25 minute drive to the airport	Anke Rice Semi Masso	74
Spain	Mallorca	Ca'n Verdera Carrer des Toros, 1 07109 Fornalutx Spain http://www.canverdera.com	opened 1998 4 double rooms, 2 suites restaurant and bar pool conference room for up to 24 people on the west coast of Mallorca, 50 km to Palma	Pepe Frontera	76
Spain	Mallorca	Ca's Xorc Carretera de Deia, km 56.1 07100 Soller Spain http://www.casxorc.com	opened 2000 10 rooms restaurant Ca's Xorc, rambling parkway pool, jacuzzi, steam bath and sauna outdoor meeting tent for up to 40 people, meeting room for 14 people in the north west of the island	Wolfgang Nikolaus Schmidt Mariano Barcelo Juan and Gregory Puigserver	78

Country	City	Address	Information	Architecture & Design	Page
Spain	Mallorca	Es Convent Progrés, 6 07400 Alcudia Spain http://www.esconvent.com	opened 2000 4 rooms restaurant Es Convent, private dining room for 14 guests located in the city centre of Alcudia	Antonio Esteva	82
Spain	Mallorca	Son Bernadinet Ctra. Campos / Porreras Km 5,9 Campos 07630 Campos Spain http://www.todoesp.es/son-bernadinet	opened 1998 11 rooms rambling garden with pool, music room in the south of Mallorca near Campos, 40 km to Palma	Antonio Esteva	84
Spain	Mallorca	Son Gener Artà, km 3 Apartat de Correus, 136 07550 Son Servera Spain http://www.todoesp.es/son-gener	opened 1998 a 18th-century manor house 10 junior suites restaurant, wine cellar swimming pool and sun terrace in the east of Mallorca, 70 km from Palma	Antonio Esteva	88
Spain	Mallorca	Son Pons 07310 Campanet-Ullaro Spain http://www.finca-son-pons.de	opened 2001 6 rooms large garden with pool in the north east of Mallorca, 30 minutes to Palma	Manfred Tumfart	94
Spain	Tenerife	San Roque Calle Esteban de Ponte 32 38450 Villa Puerto de Garachico Spain http://www.hotelsanroque.com	opened 1997 20 guest rooms including suites restaurant, patio bar swimming pool, sauna, solarium, tennis court situated in the centre of Garachico, 1 hour by car to Reina Sofia Airport	José Luis Adelantado	98
Switzerland	Laax	Riders Palace 7032 Laax Switzerland http://www.riderspalace.ch	opened 2001 71 rooms and 319 beds in 4 room types Palace Club on weekends, 24-hour bar variety of snow packages and winter events in Laax, the Alpenarena region, near mountain cable car station, 150 km from Zurich	Réne Meierhofer Arkitekt HTL/SWB	102
Switzerland	Lachen	Al Porto Hafenstr. 4 8853 Lachen / SZ Switzerland http://www.alporto.com	opened 2001 12 rooms and 5 suites ristorante "al porto", trattoria and bar banqueting and conference facilities for up to 120 people situated to the south of Lake Zurich, in Lachen	Jürg Erni Piero Lissoni Giulio Cappellini	104
Switzerland	Pontresina	Saratz Postfach 168 Laret 7504 Pontresina / St.Moritz Switzerland http://www.saratz.ch	opened 1996 92 rooms including 18 family rooms 2 restaurants, bar, cafe and hotel lobby with fireplace meeting room for up to 60 people indoor and outdoor swimming pool, wellness centre, sauna facing the Val Roseg glacier, 10 km from St. Moritz	Hans-Jörg Ruch Pia Schmid	108

Country	City	Address	Information	Architecture & Design	Page
Turkey	Ürgüp	Yunak Evleri Yunak Mahallesi 50400 Ürgüp Turkey http://www.yunakevleri.com	opened 1999 6 cave houses containing 17 rooms located in the centre of Ürgüp in Cappadocia	Cavit Kartal	112
United Kingdom	Cornwall	Hotel Tresanton 27 Lower Catle Road TR2 5DR St. Mawes United Kingdom http://www.tresanton.com	built 1940, re-opened 1999 28 bedrooms including 2 family suites restaurant, bar and lounge private 48ft racing yacht business facilities up to 60 people located close to Land's End, 80 km to Plymouth airport	Olga Polizzi	114
United Kingdom	Seaham	Seaham Hall Lord Byron's Walk SR7 7AG Seaham United Kingdom http://www.seaham-hall.com	opened 2001 18 suites and 1 penthouse gym, jacuzzi, sauna, massage, pool and beauty salon 3 conference rooms each for up to 20-30 people ballroom for events up to 100 people located between York and Edinburgh	Nappers Architects	116
United Kingdom	Somerset	Babington House Nr Frome Somerset BA11 3RW United Kingdom http://www.babingtonhouse.co.uk	opened 1999 28 rooms the "Log Room" and terrace, bar gym, sauna, 2 pools, body treatments tennis court, croquet lawn, football and cricket pitches 4 conference rooms for up to 60 people located close to Bath, 180 km to Heathrow Airport	Simon Morray-Jones	120

ARCHITECTS & INTERIOR DESIGNERS

PHOTO CREDITS

all other photos by: Martin N. Kunz

Die Deutsche Bibliothek - CIP-Data

Best designed hotels in Europe /
Martin Nicholas Kunz ; Scott Michael Crouch. - Ludwigsburg : av-Ed.

2. Countryside locations : fascinating hideaways for aesthetes. - 2002

ISBN 3-929638-89-4

Printed in Germany

Publisher | Martin Nicholas Kunz
Texts (page) | Sybille Eck (24, 38, 52, 76, 82, 114, 116),
Bärbel Holzberg (8, 10, 20, 28, 108), Saskia Lang (34, 48, 112),
Ina Sinterhauf (22, 104, 112, 120), Heinfried Tacke (30, 32, 34, 36,
74, 102)
all other texts by Martin Nicholas Kunz and Scott Michael Crouch
Translation & Editing | Nigel Geens (10, 12, 20, 28),
Vineeta Manglani (8, 34, 56, 70, 76, 83, 84, 88, 94, 112, 116, 120),
Mathis Martin (104, 114), all others by Scott M. Crouch
Research | Hanna Martin, Saskia Lang
Art Direction | Christine Rampl
Production | Markus Hartmann, Martina Weißer, Hanna Martin
Printing | Sellier Druck GmbH, Freising

Special thanks to:
Frank Bantle, riva medien, Stuttgart | Stephan Bode, Atoll Helgoland |
Francisca Bonet, Son Bernadinet | Michel Bras, Laguiole |
Norma Buckle, Hotel Tresanton | Dominique Carayon, San Roque |
Simon Carey, Villa Fontelunga | Anna Celma, Ca'n Verdera |
Miguel Angel Cortes, Es Convent | Frédéric Coustols, Castelnau Des
Fieumarcon | Andre Diogo, Estalegem da Ponta do Sol |
Pauline Engelse, Crowne Plaza Resort | Brigitte Falch, Aparthotel
Anton, St. Anton | Alicia Férnandez, Son Bernadinet |
Isabel F. Ferraz, Quinta da Casa Branca | Massimo Ferretti,
Carducci 76 | Gösta Gassmann, Ocean Drive Ibiza | Katja Hekkala,
Choupana Hills Resort | Paolo Kastelec, Villa Fontelunga |
Regine Lieberuks, Seehotel Neuklostersee |
Christiane und Edelbert Lösch, Kloster Hornbach | Maison Coté Sud |
Gill McFadden, Seaham Hall | Philippe Moreau, Choupana Hills
Resort | Olivier Spinner | Johanne und Gernot Nalbach,
Seehoel Neuklostersee | Okan Ozdizdar, Yunak Evleri |
Britta Plönzke, Ca's Xorc | Eric Raffy | Philipp Robinson,
Villa Fontelunga | Diniz Madaleno Rodrigues, Farol Design Hotel |
Bettina Römer, al porto | Kay Schröder, Camp Reinsehlen |
Angelika Senger, Son Gener | Gerd Spans, The Good Life GmbH |
Adrian Stalder, Saratz | Katharina Stinnes-Mauch, Schlosshotel
Lütgenhof | Anja Ullmann, Riders Palace | Barbara Widera,
Babington House | Ingrid, Astrid und Christian Wolter, Son Pons

lebensart global networks AG – division publishing
Konrad-Adenauer-Allee 35-37 | 86150 Augsburg | Germany
p +49-821-34545-928 | f +49-821-34545-925

publishing@lebensart-ag.com | http://www.lebensart-ag.com

avedition GmbH
Königsallee 57 | 71638 Ludwigsburg | Germany
p +49-7141-1477-391 | f +49-7141-1477-399

kontakt@avedition.de | http://www.avedition.de